Contents

DR. ROBERT G. COLLIER

Perceptual Training
Activities Handbook

Also by Betty Van Witsen:

Teaching Children with Severe Behavior/Communication Disorders

PERCEPTUAL TRAINING ACTIVITIES HANDBOOK

250 Games and Exercises
for Helping Children Develop Sensory Skills

Second Edition

Betty Van Witsen

Learning Disability Teacher, Hewlett-Woodmere Schools, N.Y., and
Adjunct Associate Professor of Special Education,
Fordham University

Teachers College, Columbia University
New York 1979

Illustrations by Roxana Wright Rogers

Cover and Text Design by Romeo M. Enriquez

Cover "Mystery Picture": Courtesy of Optometric Extension Program
Foundation, Inc., Duncan, OK 73533

Figure 1, activity 172: Reprinted by permission of S. G. Phillips,
Inc. from *How to Raise Your Child's I.Q.* by David Engler. Copyright
© 1958 by S. G. Phillips, Inc.

Library of Congress Cataloging in Publication Data

Van Witsen, Betty.
  Perceptual training activities handbook.

  Bibliography: p.
  Includes index.
  1. Perceptual learning. 2. Teachers of
handicapped children, Training of—United States.
I. Title.
LC4031.V3 1979   371.9   79-17371
ISBN 0-8077-2568-4

Manufactured in the United States of America

10 9 8 7 6 5 4 3 2 1   79 80 81 82 83 84

Foreword

Betty Van Witsen has again responded to teachers' requests for assistance in planning and implementing programs for their pupils who are encountering difficulty in accomplishing some of the usual school tasks. She has effectively updated and augmented the instructional activities which have, for over a decade, proven to be helpful to teachers and parents.

The timeliness of the activities is evident as teachers and educational supervisors work to prepare and carry out individualized program plans (IEP's) as mandated in PL 94–142, the Education of all Handicapped Children Act. From the practice materials herein presented, specific activities can easily be selected for specific children. Also, modifications in form and content can be made as diagnostic information and reports on student performance emerge.

The practice activities, often appearing as games or puzzles, are attractive and natural for children, both handicapped and non-handicapped. They are based upon current knowledge about children, their interests, their ways of learning and some of the known impediments to such learning. The author has made no claims of direct correlation between a designated learning or behavioral disability and one or more of the activities herein described Although the material is not research-based, it is well tested by in-service teachers who have validated the activities through use with children in all parts of the United States and in many countries throughout the world.

The author's obvious skill in analyzing tasks performed by children as they live and grow in usual child environments facilitates the reader's comprehension of the activities as described and the subsequent use of them with children who need help in their learning. This publication reflects the knowledge, skill, and experience of a gifted teacher and teacher educator: one whose classroom activities take advantage of a child's curiosity and of childrens' desires to achieve (or to "win") and to enjoy the challenges and processes of learning.

FRANCES P. CONNOR
Chairman, Department of Special Education
Teachers College, Columbia University

Preface to the Second Edition

More than thirteen years have passed since the first publication of *Perceptual Training Activities Handbook*. The first edition was reprinted nine times, giving ample evidence of the need for the kind of material it offers.

In these thirteen years the general acceptance and appreciation of the value of perceptual training has become almost universal among teachers, parents, therapists, optometrists, psychologists, and other groups of people who work directly with children. They use perceptual training activities to enhance, refine, and provide practice for developmental sensory skills that both precede and accompany the more mature skills of literacy.

Developmental skills are those that develop naturally as a child gets older, for example walking and talking. They develop spontaneously. The skills of literacy (reading, writing, and arithmetic, to name the three most basic ones) are also considered developmental in a sense: with instruction and guidance, most children who have matured sufficiently can learn them easily and naturally. Not all children, however, mature sufficiently at the same age, and not all children mature sufficiently in an even, regular way.

Knowledgeable teachers are aware that perceptual training activities will not teach a child to read or to do arithmetic. They realize that some children, moreover, develop what have been called splinter skills, skills operative on a higher developmental level than that of sensory perception before related lower-level skills are developed.

The activities in this book, however, provide practice (enjoyable gamelike practice) in the natural skills of sensory awareness; and with repeated practice children develop ease, flexibility, and confidence in sensory functions. People who do puzzles learn to become good and efficient puzzle-doers. If the puzzles deal with space, as with jigsaw puzzles, such people develop facility in recognizing and matching irregular shapes. For this facility to be used in other contexts, however (e.g., sorting parts in a workshop), provision must be made for the transfer of the skill. If the puzzles deal with words, as in crossword puzzles, the people who do them develop facility in finding synonyms and in mentally scanning their vocabularies to find words that fit definitions. For this facility to be used in other situations (e.g., understanding words in the context of reading), provision has to be made for the transfer of this skill. Skills that have been practiced seem to be more readily transferred than skills in which little or no practice has occurred.

Many children provide themselves with practice through spontaneous play. Many other children—those with disabilities of the central nervous system, those with emotional problems, those with language backgrounds that are significantly different from that expected of school-age children, or those with developmental disabilities that retard natural practice in sensory awareness and language—cannot do this without help.

In this second edition, *Perceptual Training Activities Handbook* has been substantially expanded, particularly in language and body-image activities. The bibliography has been revised and updated; it includes a variety of sources of developmental skill learning activities, not limited to books referred to in the text.

I hope this new edition of *PTAH* (not an Egyptian god, but this volume) will be helpful to teachers in providing varied activities to enhance children's learning.

B.V.W.

Perceptual Training
Activities Handbook

"Mystery" Picture. Reprinted courtesy of the Optometric Extension Program
Foundation, Inc., Duncan, OK 73533

1
Introduction

Perception is the interpretation of sensation. It is based upon previous experience of sensations, through interaction with the environment. Perception, then, is a learned function, and as a learned function it is susceptible to teaching. This teaching can be accomplished through the provision of planned sensory experiences (together with the interpretation of such experiences to the child) in vision, language, gesture, kinesthesis, and touch. An example of an ambiguous picture, which one can *see* clearly but must *learn* to *perceive*, faces this page. (To learn to perceive it, see pages 94-95.)

The activities suggested in this book are divided into functional aspects of the different sensory modes: vision, hearing, touch, smell, taste, and kinesthesis, or muscle-sense. Perception of sensations, or understanding of the meaning of sensations, depends to some extent on the integration of the various senses, so that the message that is conveyed is reinforced. For example, most children soon learn that a particular sight (steam rising from a cup, brown liquid in the cup), a particular tactile sensation (heat in the fingers holding the cup), a particular odor in the nostrils as the cup is raised to the lips, and a particular taste as the liquid is taken into the mouth, all mean that the contents of the cup is hot chocolate. One learns this, however, after one has drunk hot chocolate, and has heard the words "hot chocolate" as one looks at the liquid, tastes it, smells it, and feels the heat.

Some children cannot sort out these sensations—they become confused by what they see, hear, taste, smell, feel. One sense does not reinforce the message that another sense conveys. Such children may not be able to integrate their sensory experiences into a meaningful perception; they frequently exhibit peculiar behavior: disorganization, impulsivity, perseveration, disinhibition, distractibility, figure-ground confusion.

Whether this behavior is the *cause* of their learning difficulties, the *result* of perceptual confusion, or simply *associated* with it appears to be irrelevant; the important thing is that such behavior seems to be amenable to modification by management techniques on the part of the teacher. The perceptual training activities in this book have been used and recommended by teachers of

1

children with different kinds of learning difficulties. These teachers have found that as the child learns to understand sensations, and to organize experiences into meaningful phenomena, behavior frequently improves. The activities can be used with a wide range of children and with a wide range of learning problems. They have not been designed specifically for children with peripheral nervous-system involvement, although some of them might be adapted for hard-of-hearing and deaf children, and for visually handicapped and blind children. In all cases, the objectives and activities used should be in keeping with the children's experience and interests.

In addition to the general perceptual training activities presented in this book, a number of suggestions from the literature that have been found helpful in bringing behavioral problems within the child's control are described and discussed in Chapter 2.

2
Behavior Problems

Behavior	Description	Management Techniques
Disorganization	The child appears unable to carry out a task or to pay attention to the material at hand in an orderly fashion. His responses appear to be random and meaningless. This behavior is frequently accompanied by personal untidiness, meaningless arrangement of materials in the child's desk, and lack of even rudimentary planning in either self-directed activities or teacher-directed tasks.	Highly structured routines and specific instructions are needed. The child should receive increased individual attention, decreased peripheral stimulation, explicit directions for each step of the learning process, short tasks—each with a clear end in sight, and a reward for each correct response.
Distractibility	The child's attention cannot remain focused. He appears to be at the mercy of every passing stimulus, even ones that would go unnoticed as usual background phenomena by normal children, such as the rustling of the blinds or the sight of the teacher's wristwatch.	Brightly colored instructional material, having a clear, specific purpose, may be used to engage the child's attention. He should be assigned a single task of short duration, initially, and the material must be put away immediately after use.

Behavior	Description	Management Techniques
Perseveration	The child is unable to shift attention or to change behavior that is no longer appropriate. In some ways this appears as the opposite of distractibility, but it is not really, since the child is not truly concentrating his attention—he is responding automatically with a previously successful response, despite its irrelevance. "The needle gets stuck in the groove."	Physical separation of each individual image (word, picture, or figure) by lines or cardboard strips or by use of cardboard cut-out devices, helps define each image for the child. Different colors can heighten the child's awareness of the need for different responses. A change of material presenting the same problem can sometimes get a child over the hurdle of perseveration. It is sometimes helpful to change the child's physical position in the room, either by moving his desk and chair, or by having him change from a seated position to a standing one.
Dissociation or Figure-Ground Confusion	The child cannot pull a stimulus from its background in any sensory mode. Visually, this means, for example, that he cannot understand a picture, because he confuses the outlines of it with the background of the picture. Auditorily, he cannot shut out background noises from the sounds he is supposed to be listening to or trying to listen to. It is not that he is distracted, for that implies that he shifts his attention; rather he incorporates the background material into	Heavy outlining of the visual figure presented is frequently helpful in enabling the child to perceive and focus on a particular image. Framing the various parts of a picture with a cardboard cut-out is sometimes effective. Use of two-piece teacher-made puzzles, then three-piece puzzles, in which the picture is taken apart and then put together again, helps the child learn to pull apart and put together various parts of an image, physically at first, then in his imagination. For auditory

Behavior	Description	Management Techniques

| | the foreground, thus losing the meaning of the stimulus. | confusion problems, it is sometimes helpful to talk directly to the child through an improvised paper megaphone. |

| **Impulsivity and Disinhibition** | The child exhibits an unplanned action or motor response that appears meaningless and inappropriate to the apparent stimulus. Sometimes that is referred to as "forced motor response." The child appears to be directed by his own need for motor activity, and impervious to the actual demands of the situation. | Materials which exploit a purposeful motor reaction—pegs, sorting boxes, crayons, clay pans in which to write with a stylus, toothpicks inserted into a salt shaker top—all help the child refrain from irrelevant motor behavior. It is necessary to give specific directions for the use of these devices and materials, and sometimes even for the use and placement of the child's hands when they are temporarily idle. It is important to avoid having unnecessary materials within reach of the child, or even within his visual reach. Closed cupboards for storing material not in use are essential for controlling this kind of behavior. |

| **Hyperactivity** | A child, particularly a young child, is observed to dash about madly, picking up one object after another, tossing it aside for the next one, sometimes talking incessantly, asking myriad questions and not waiting for answers. The child appears to be unable to focus | Screening a child off from the rest of the room is sometimes effective in helping him to control his hyperactivity, and is also helpful in controlling distractibility. Screening, however, should *never* be associated with punishment. It should be presented, rather, as a "pri- |

5

| | his attention on anything for more than a second or two. | vate office" in which the child will not be bothered by other children. The child should always be assigned a particular task to do when he is in his office—he should not daydream or remain idle. The assigned tasks should be well within the child's capabilities, and they appear to be most effective when they require a motor response, for example sorting shapes, tracing lines, or arranging pegs in a peg board. The hyperactivity is thus narrowed down and channeled into useful pathways. |
| **Catastrophic Reaction** | The child exhibits an overflow of response, or a sudden collapse of controls for no apparent reason, and to a degree seemingly unwarranted by the stimulus. His confusion about the world is such that anything out of the ordinary can appear threatening, even terrifying. For such a child, a dropped crayon can be paralyzing or can cause him to burst into tears. | Strongly structured routines, multi-sensory approaches to learning, or focus toward a designated unisensory approach (such as the use of earphones), concrete materials, and meaningful situations can help the child organize himself so that he is less likely to panic in new situations. He needs to be reassured frequently that everyone makes mistakes, and that mistakes can be corrected. When he does lose control, it is helpful to let him go to his "office" with a book or some other nonthreatening activity that can help him to organize himself. A calm demeanor |

Behavior	Description	Management Techniques
		on the part of the teacher, and a friendly pat on the shoulder, can help him see the episode in proper perspective.
Concrete Behavior	The child is unable to generalize or is unaware of different aspects of an object, word, or idea. For example, if told to punch a hole in a paper, he might make the hole with the hole punch, then carefully double up his fist and punch it. This phenomenon, quite natural to very young children, sometimes persists for a long time in children with learning disabilities. Another example of concrete behavior is evidenced by the child who cannot grasp the fact that the color pink could be considered as a variation of red. To him, pink is an entirely different color.	The strongest sensory channel should be used to support the weaker ones. Which channel is strongest can best be determined by careful observation on the part of the teacher. Games of categorization and grouping, such as card games at first and later more difficult games (suggested later in this book), can help the child appreciate classification principles so that every phenomenon does not appear as separate and distinct to him. Natural language and natural situations can be exploited in this area with much success—actual life situations seem to be more helpful to the child with this problem than artificial ones. For example, in discussing families, the teacher can point out that everyone is a "Jones," although each one is a separate person. Games of "how they are alike" or "how they are different" also help the child with this problem.

7

3
Teaching

Certain recognized principles of teaching apply to all levels of learning, whether regular or special, nursery school or college, and these should be borne in mind by all teachers. Some of these concern psychological aspects of human development, some the structure of subject matter. Learning has been defined as modification of behavior through experience, involving growth as a response to stimulation, and dependent upon the intent or the will to learn, or motivation.

For the child with learning disabilities, there is frequently a history of failure, confusion, negative self-image, and fear of school learning. Difficult as it may be to renew the child's natural desire to learn, this desire must be present or the teacher's task becomes insuperable.

In beginning to teach a child with learning disabilities, it is wise for the teacher to limit the stimuli in order to focus the child's attention on a particular object or task. The teacher must also *structure the situation* for the child, that is, present the material in such a way that the goals and the necessary behavior are clearly defined and the procedure is built in a step-by-step sequence. One cannot take for granted that the child understands what is required of him—on the contrary, he frequently does not. For example, a normal child, when told by his teacher to put his book away in his desk, can do so. A child with learning disabilities might need to be told, "Close your book. Now put it in your desk."

Activities that the child is willing to participate in must, at the beginning, be immediately rewarding *in terms of the activities themselves*. Praise from the teacher quickly becomes routine and meaningless if it is bestowed too generously on every occasion. Genuine concern and affection for the child will become apparent to him, but his every effort should not be overpraised if he is to learn the value of an activity for its ultimate meaning for him, rather than as a means of pleasing the teacher.

Freidus has mentioned six aspects of learning, each of which must be handled adequately by the child if he is to achieve positive results. These steps constitute a good checklist for the teacher in beginning to work with a child with learning disabilities.

1. Sensory stimulus (Can the child see, hear; is his sensory equipment intact?)
2. Voluntary focus (Can he pay attention, or is he too distracted by other stimuli, either external or internal?)
3. Understanding (Can he understand what is required of him—does he *perceive* the task?)
4. Intended response (Does he know what he ought to do about it?)
5. Organizing and performing (Can he mobilize himself and make a response?)
6. Feedback (Can he check and know whether he has done what he set out to do?)[1]

There is no one "correct" method of teaching reading, writing, or arithmetic—effective methods abound in the teachers' manuals of most regular basal reading, arithmetic, and writing series. Many teachers invent their own methods. What is important is that the teacher have a very clear idea of what he wants the child to learn, that he present it in logical order, from simple to complex, that he give the child ample practice in activities that the child can enjoy and see the value of, and that both the child and the teacher (not to mention the child's parents) be aware of growth and progress. As the child learns to trust his own capabilities, he can develop self-respect and ego-strength—qualities that are tragically lacking in many children with learning disabilities.

---

[1] Elizabeth Freidus, lecture delivered at Teachers College, Columbia University, Spring, 1960.

4
Visual Training and Small Motor Skills

Vision is a complex process involving more than sharpness of image:

> Efficiency and meaning-getting are reduced if the eye cannot follow what it is supposed to look at, if it cannot switch easily and accurately from one point to another, if the two eyes cannot work in harmony as a team to focus and center on what it should be directed on, or if the eyes need other senses such as finger touch, head movements, or vocalization to help the elements in the visual process function better. Visual abilities are all motor skills, and as such are strongly influenced by the motor ability of the body in general.[2]

Visual perception activities include eye-movement and focus activities, form perception activities, visual memory activities, visual comparison activities, visual conceptualization activities, and eye-hand coordination activities. The emphasis is on the functional rather than the medical aspects of vision.

EYE MOVEMENT AND FOCUSING

1. Sit in front of the child with four or five small familiar objects on your lap. Pick up one with your right hand and hold it off to the child's left side. Ask the child to look at it and name it. While his attention is on the object, pick up another one with your left hand and hold it to his right side. Ask him to look at this and name it. Repeat. Keep going as long as possible, with quick change of objects. After some practice, try to produce rapid eye movement and less head movement in all directions. The objects used in this game should be unique and not used for any other purpose, so that the child can maintain a high interest level. For older, more sophisticated children, do not use toys, but rather tools, car

---

[2] Elliot B. Forrest, personal communication.

miniatures, plane models, letters and numbers (if familiar), flash cards of familiar words, and so on, giving a dual purpose to the game.

2. Hand things to children from various angles and positions so that they must look at and reach for them.

3. *Rollaround Ball.*[3] Use a large ring-shaped gelatin mold and a ping pong ball. Hold the mold with the ball in it, and tilt it so that the ball rolls rhythmically around it. Have the child follow the movement of the ball, without moving his head if possible. Reverse the direction of the ball occasionally.

4. *"Marsden Ball."*[4] A ball, 2 inches in diameter, with a string through it, is hung from a hook in the ceiling or a doorway, or from a tree branch outdoors.
   A. Place the ball so that it is at the child's eye level when he stands facing it. Swing it gently to and from him and have him watch it as it comes and goes. He may need to point with his finger at first.
   B. Swing the ball from side to side, and have the child perform the activity described in A, above.
   C. Suspend the ball about three feet from the floor. Have the child lie on his back directly under it. Swing it in large circles and ask the child to watch it until it comes to a stop. It may be necessary to paint a red spot on the ball for the child to focus on.

5. Have the child hold right and left forefingers up in front of him, 12 to 14 inches apart and about 12 inches away from his eyes. Put a thimble or finger puppet on each finger. Have him look quickly from left to right and from right to left. Be sure his eyes land on the target each time. If there is difficulty, the teacher can use his own index finger to touch the child's fingers, or a pencil to make a click on each thimble for auditory reinforcement, to pace the child's eyes.

6. Have the child hold a pencil erect 10 to 12 inches in front of his nose. Have him look from the pencil to a wall or chalkboard picture and back to the pencil as quickly as possible. Make ten or fifteen round trips, and be sure that he sees both targets clearly and quickly. Then move the pencil nearer to his nose. This exercise helps the child develop flexibility of focus.

7. *Flashlight Game.* The teacher shines a flashlight on the chalkboard, and the child catches the light with his own flashlight. The teacher then moves his light and the child follows it and catches it with his light. Move in a

---

[3] G. N. Getman, *How to Develop Your Child's Intelligence* (Luverne, Minn.: Author, 1958).
[4] *Ibid.*

11

circle at first, then in horizontal, vertical, and oblique directions. Stop each time your light is caught to fix the child's eyes on it. Aim for rapid movement on the part of the child. When the child becomes familiar with this game, two children can play it together, one following the other's light.

A more sophisticated version of this would be for the "teacher" to move in a particular pattern (circle, cross, letter, square, etc.), and for the follower to guess the pattern after the end of the activity by drawing it. This is good for visual memory and visual projection, and complicated enough to interest older students, if complex patterns are used.

8. *"Wall Baseball."*[5] Put large colored circles, far apart, on one clear wall of the room. (Later on, they can be all one color and be numbered differently, but at first use colors as the cue.) The children stand at the other end of the room. They are instructed to look at each color named without moving their heads. After some practice (i.e., as soon as they know where the colors are) the game starts. One at a time, the children "come up to bat." If the child's eyes miss the target or skip it, he has a "strike" against him. Three strikes and he's out! Completing the routine is a "home run." The teacher must watch the children's eye movements, having memorized where the colors are.

A. *Practice routine.* Call the colors in this order: *red, blue, yellow—black, green, pink—white, orange, brown.* If any difficulty is noted, touch each color with a pointer at first as it is called. If the difficulty persists, have the child point with his outstretched arm and forefinger.

B. *Game.* With each child, call each of these sequences *twice,* until the child strikes out or makes a home run:

Red, yellow, white, brown
Red, yellow, black, pink, white, brown
Red, blue, black, green, white, orange
Blue, yellow, orange, brown
Blue, yellow, green, pink, orange, brown

RED   BLUE   YELLOW

BLACK   GREEN   PINK

WHITE   ORANGE   BROWN

FORM PERCEPTION

At age four most children can perceive a circle, a square, and a vertical line crossed by a horizontal line; at five they can perceive a triangle; at six, a diamond; at seven, a rectangle with a vertical-horizontal cross superimposed over an oblique cross and a horizontally oriented diamond.

[5] Elliott B. Forrest, personal communication.

Stencils

Stencils are sometimes called templates.

9. The teacher makes two sets of stencils, using cardboards about 8 inches square, of a circle, square, equilateral triangle, horizontally oriented rectangle, vertically oriented rectangle, and horizontally and vertically oriented diamonds. Set 1 should consist of the solid shape. Set 2, then, is the frame with the shape cut out of it (the bottom edge should be black, to orient the child). The child traces both kinds of stencils at the chalkboard. Meaning should be associated with each shape.

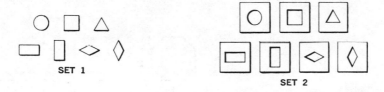

10. The child uses similar stencils, but only 4 inches square, and traces them on paper at a desk or table, naming the shape and associating meaning with it.

11. The child colors the shape within the stencil frame.

12. The child colors the traced shape without the aid of the stencil.

13. Two shapes are combined, and meaning is associated with the resulting figure (e.g., triangle + circle = ice cream cone).

ICE CREAM CONE   HOUSE

14. More than two shapes are combined, and meaning is associated with the result.

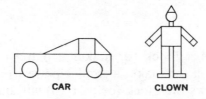

CAR   CLOWN

Peg Boards[6]

15. Follow stencils on the peg board.
   - A. Horizontal line
   - B. Vertical line
   - C. Square
   - D. Rectangle
   - E. Triangle
   - F. Parallelogram
   - G. Trapezoid
   - H. Hexagon
   - I. Octagon
   - J. Diamond
   - K. Cross
   - L. X
   - M. Star

16. After the child can follow all the shapes in §15 using stencils, have him copy the single forms, without the stencil.

17. Have the child copy designs that combine stencil forms.

18. Have the child copy letters.

ELHAT

19. Have the child copy more complicated figures, with meaning (house, boat, etc.).

HOUSE   BOAT   TREE   CHAIR

Parquetry Blocks[7]

20. The teacher selects a block (or makes a pattern of blocks). The child picks a similar block (or makes a similar pattern) and traces it on paper. Then the child draws the block (or pattern) without tracing.

---

[6] Isaac M. Jolles, "A Teaching Sequence for Training Visual and Motor Perception," *American Journal of Mental Deficiency*, 1958, 63: 252-255.

[7] *Ibid.*

14

A. Single square.
B. Combination of squares to make a big square.
C. Single diamond.
D. Combination of diamonds.
E. Single triangle
F. Combination of triangles.
G. Combine two forms.
H. Combine more than two forms.

I. Combine forms into meaningful pictures (sailboat, flower, airplane, etc.).
J. Leave the color out of the picture to be drawn.
K. Make the lines between the shapes lighter.
L. Leave out the lines that define the different shapes.

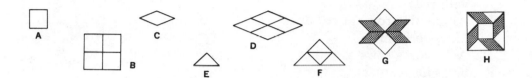

21. The child designs his own patterns, working directly with the parquetry blocks, then copies the design on paper.

22. Apply the designs and patterns to functional material; for example, have children make a book cover, a birthday card, posters, book plates, gift paper, and so on. This kind of activity can be encouraged by having a class collection of good advertising art that uses basic forms, so that the children can see the application of what they have learned.

Design Blocks

Design blocks are cubes that have four faces of different colors and two faces divided into two triangles of different colors.

23. The child copies designs formed by laying out one layer of blocks on a flat surface.
    A. Single red block.
    B. Single red and single blue, horizontally oriented.
    C. Single red and single blue, vertically oriented.

    D. Single red, single blue, and single yellow, horizontally oriented.
    E. Single red, single blue, and single yellow, vertically oriented.
    F. Single red, bounded on four sides with single yellows.

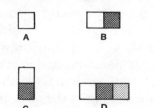

(*continued*)

G

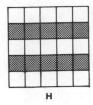

H

I

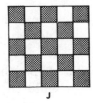

J

G. Fill the box, or a frame, with reds.

H. Alternating rows of red and blue, horizontal.

I. Alternating rows of yellow and blue, vertical.

J. Red and blue checkerboard pattern.

K. More complicated patterns of single colors.

L. Combinations of divided-face patterns.

M. Use designs furnished with the blocks.

Popstick Patterns

24. "Popsticks" are flat wooden sticks like the ones from ice cream bars. The teacher lays out a design using ten popsticks. Children must match the pattern. Children can take turns laying out patterns. The patterns can be either two-dimensional or three-dimensional; that is, the teacher or a child may build up a pattern by putting sticks on top of sticks. The winner is the one who can copy the most patterns.

Dot Game

25. Dots are drawn on a piece of paper in the form of a square: the same number of dots across as down (any number desired). Players take turns connecting dots with straight lines. (Usually two people play this game, but more can compete by using different colored pencils or markers.) Players may connect only two dots at a time. The object is to complete as many squares or boxes as possible, by making the fourth side. When a player completes a box, he puts his initials in it and may draw another line, continuing until he draws a line that does *not* make a box. The winner is the player with the most boxes with his initials in them. This game can be varied by making triangles or rectangles the goal, instead of square boxes.

16

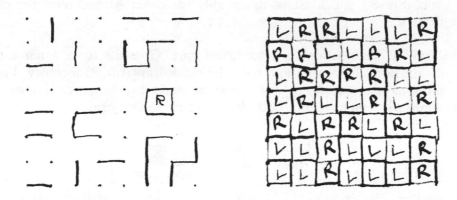

VISUAL MEMORY

26. Place several familiar toys or objects on a table behind the child, or have him sit with his back to his desk. Tell him to look at the objects for a few seconds, then turn away and name as many objects as he can remember. Start with three objects and gradually increase the number.

27. Place four objects on a table. Have the child close his eyes while you remove one object. Then ask him to look and tell what is missing. Sometimes naming the objects, or having the child name them before the game begins, helps him to remember them. Increase the number of objects. When the number is more than six, select objects that can be associated in pairs (big and little shells, knife and fork, pencil and chalk, etc.). Teach the child to associate them, so that he has a clue as to what to look for. When nine or more objects are used, try to associate them in threes.

A variation on this game is the selection of random objects and a discussion of how one could arrange them, that is, what goes with what. Classification criteria must be pointed out to the children (e.g., shape, color, function, material, size). Use only one criterion at a time.

Some children become very skillful at this game, and some, of course, have considerable difficulty in shifting from one criterion to another. Keep the objects simple and select objects with very noticeable characteristics at first.

This is good practice both in visual memory and in organization skill. Teach the application of this skill, once it is attained, in other, more abstract, areas of memory.

28. Expose a picture showing many familiar objects. Cover it and have the child tell as many things as he remembers seeing.

29. Draw a simple form or pattern on the chalkboard while the child watches

17

you. Erase it quickly and thoroughly (or cover it) and have the child draw it.

30. Draw a combination of geometric forms. Give the form a name (see illustration). Remove it and have the child draw it from memory. Later, omit naming the form; just show the child the form for a moment, remove it, and have him both draw and name the form.

31. *"Tic-Tac-Toe-Tachistoscope."*[8] The teacher draws a tic-tac-toe frame on the chalkboard. The children copy it on their papers. The teacher then puts an X or an O in one box, exposing it for two seconds, then covering it. The children then put the symbol on their patterns in the same space. Begin with one symbol, increase to two or three, and speed the exposure time. You may have to begin by structuring the spaces in the pattern verbally for some children (left, middle, right; top, bottom, center; left top, middle top, etc.).

LEFT TOP	MIDDLE TOP	RIGHT TOP
MIDDLE LEFT	CENTER	MIDDLE RIGHT
LEFT BOTTOM	MIDDLE BOTTOM	RIGHT BOTTOM

32. The teacher lines up a series of objects, pictures, or toys on the table. The children are told to look carefully at them. Then, while they close their eyes, the teacher shifts the order by moving one object. A child is called on to replace it in the correct order. Later, the teacher can shift two or three objects.

33. *Scrambled Eggs.* This game is for a group of ten to twenty youngsters. One child puts his head down and closes his eyes. The others all change places, except one, who leaves the room. The child who is "It" then must guess who left the room.

34. *Follow Touch.* The teacher walks around the room and touches an object. The first child touches the same object, then walks around and touches something else. The second child touches the two previously touched

---

[8] Elliott B. Forrest, personal communication.

objects, in order, then walks around the room and touches a third object, and so forth. The object of the game is to remember the sequence of objects touched. Anyone who forgets an object or touches one out of order drops out of the game. The winner is the last person in the game.

35. *Change-O*. Each child takes a partner. One partner closes his eyes or turns his back while the other partner changes something about the way he looks (removes a wrist watch, unties a shoe, pulls off his sweater, puts on glasses, rolls up one pants leg) and the other partner must discover what change has been made.

VISUAL COMPARISON

The following activities provide practice in recognition of likenesses and differences in size, shape, color, texture, position, and meaning.

Jigsaw Puzzles

36. The child reorganizes a picture of a face cut into three parts, or a symmetrical object (e.g., a bottle or a ball) cut in half, or an asymmetrical object (e.g., an animal) cut in half.

37. The child reorganizes a picture cut into several parts, after seeing the whole picture first. Sometimes he needs a duplicate of the whole picture to refer to, initially.

38. Use very simple commercial puzzles, in which each piece is a separate object, separated from the other pieces by solid background space.

39. Use commercial puzzles in which the objects pictured are composed of several pieces, each piece having logical boundaries. Teachers can make this kind of puzzle, which helps in body-image also.

40. Use more complicated puzzles, in which there is no logic in the boundaries of the pieces but in which the picture is relatively uncomplicated and the pieces are large.

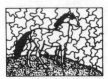

41. Adult puzzles may be worked on by the group as a form of recreation.

Matching and Sorting

Various Things

42. Cut geometric shapes of various colors. Have the child match them as to shape, then as to color, then as to size. Begin with circles and squares, then add triangles, rectangles, diamonds, parallelograms, trapezoids, hexagons, and octagons. Let the child sort these by matching into various boxes. Begin with two contrasting forms, then increase to four or five.

43. Sorting concrete objects that go together:
                    Silverware, crayons, pencils, and books.
                    Papers according to size.
                    Teacher's stationery supplies.

Pictures

44. *Animal Pictures.* The teacher presents three animal pictures, for example two cats and one dog. The children are asked to point to the one that is different. Other classifications, such as vegetables, or houses, can be used. Gradually increase the fineness of the distinctions.

45. *Teacher-prepared Material.* The teacher cuts pictures from magazines and mounts on tagboard. The child sorts the pictures using function as a criterion. Pictures may be of tools, fruits, vehicles, toys, birds, children, etc.

46. *Commercial Material.* "Play Store" and "Play House" (available from Creative Playthings) are useful in this kind of activity. Card games such as "Old Maid" and "Picture Rummy," available at stationery stores, are also good for grouping concepts.

47. *Catalog Hunt.* A store catalog, such as Sears' or Montgomery Ward's or Spiegel's, is used to find objects that go together. For younger children, the teacher might remove the appropriate pages for use. With more advanced children, the index can be used. The teacher introduces the activity by telling a short narrative about the category, and presenting the problem to be solved. For example: "My cousin is going on a fishing trip. She needs to take some things with her. What can you find for her to take along?" Some other situations for narratives are listed below:

Going to the country	A sick friend	Visiting Grandma
Traveling to Europe	A birthday party	A garden
Going in the Army	A kitchen shower	A new house
A guest coming to stay	Going to college	Christmas
A day at the beach	Repairing the sink	A wedding
A new baby	Going to the city	Animals
Camping out	Starting school	

48. *Picture Dominoes,* commercial or teacher-made of 2-inch by 4-inch strips of cardboard, divided into 2-by-2 inch squares. The symbols used on each strip (two to a strip) can be pictures of objects or they can be abstract shapes such as circles, squares, triangles, stars, diamonds.

49. *Picture Lotto,* commercial or teacher-made. The pictures can be of animals or objects in a particular category, for example, food, flowers, toys, clothing, vehicles, household objects. A variation on this is cards using symbols, each card using one form and the six pictures on it being different uses of the form. For example, the "circle" card could have pictures of the sun, a ball, a face, a balloon, a clock, and a lollypop; the "square" card could have a window, a box, a table, a book, a house, a piece of candy.

50. *Picture Stories.* A large sheet or strip of oaktag is divided into four (or five or six) sections. In each section there is a picture showing some phase of an activity or sequence that is shown completed in the last picture. The same pictures are also placed on individual small cards (the same size as the sections of the large sheet). The child takes the small pictures and assembles them to tell the same story as that on the large sheet.

Later, when the child is proficient at this, let him assemble small pictures to tell a story without referring to a guide sheet.

Buttons, Beads, and Toothpicks

51. *Stringing Beads.* Use large nursery beads of different shapes. Have the child sort them first as to shape, then string them following a pattern. When he becomes adept at this, the size of the beads can be reduced, then various shapes of macaroni, colored with food coloring, can be used. Organizing this kind of material into boxes according to color or size or shape (depending on the activity the teacher has in mind) is good experience.

52. *Sort the Buttons.* The teacher obtains a large collection of different kinds of buttons. Children sort them into egg cartons by specified criteria. Some of the criteria might be number of holes, color, size, shank vs. no shank.

53. *Follow the Colors.* An empty onion-salt container can be used for eye-hand coordination activities. Color around the holes in the plastic shaker top in different patterns, and have the children match the colors by inserting colored toothpicks into the holes.

Dominoes

54. Regular domino games are played as follows: The first player sets a double (a domino with the same number on both ends), and after that each player must match one or another open end. The player getting rid of his dominoes first is the winner. At the beginning of the game, the dominoes are placed face down and stirred around. Each player then takes seven dominoes. When a player cannot match an open end from the dominoes in his hand, he goes to the "bone-yard" and draws until he gets a domino he can use, until there are only two dominoes left in the bone-yard. If one player gets rid of all his dominoes, his score is the value of the pips in the opponents' hands. If no more moves can be made, the winning score is the difference between the score of the lowest hand and the sum of the other scores.

Copying and Illustrating

55. Have the child copy his first initial, then his whole name, in block capital letters. Later add other letters of the alphabet, and words. If he cannot copy, let him trace the letters at first.

56. Put hand-lettered labels on various objects in the room (*desk, window, door, chair, book, eraser,. . .*). Give the child a corresponding set of labels

and have him go about the room matching them to the objects. Begin with one or two very different-looking words, and increase in number and difficulty of labels.

Later, let the child copy each label from the object label. When he can do it well, and remembers the words, remove the labels and have him put on paper the word for the object, then the word for pictures of the objects, then use only the spoken word as a cue.

57. Have the child draw pictures and tell about the drawing.

58. Have the child draw pictures to illustrate a story.

59. Have the child tell a story of his own experience. Make a booklet of the story. Let the child illustrate it and "read" it from memory.

VISUAL CONCEPTUALIZATION

Visual conceptualization, as the term is used here, means imaginative or eidetic thinking. The following activities in imaginative thinking require the use of memory and visual comparison.

60. Describe something and have the child name it from your description. (E.g.: "I am thinking of something big and yellow, with a door and four wheels and windows all around, that is used to go places.") The child first names it. Later he can add details of his own. This game can be played by a group, each child adding descriptive details until everyone recognizes the object by verbal description.

61. Describe the clothes and appearance of a person in the school until the child can tell who is being described. Let the child describe someone and let the other children guess who it is.

62. Describe a place, using the same technique as in §61.

63. Have the child tell about a trip to the store with his mother. Question, and lead him into details of the store and its contents. Let other children guess what kind of store it was.

64. Have the child tell about a television commercial without naming the product advertised, merely describing the activity. Let the other children guess the product, and tell what kind of store one would buy it at.

65. Have the child tell in detail how he gets from his house to someone else's

house, or have him describe the bus trip to and from school: what he passes, what kind of road the bus goes on, details of traffic conditions, and so on.

66. *"Where Is It?"* Have the child close his eyes and point to various people and objects in the room as they are named. If he makes an error he opens his eyes.

67. Ask the child to get something in the room, but before he does, have him describe exactly where it is, without pointing (in the teacher's top desk drawer, at the back of the room, on the bottom shelf, etc.).

68. *Store Windows.* The child is taken on a walking trip, perhaps by his parents. He studies a store window, then walks away and tries to remember as many items in the window as possible. This can be varied by using detailed pictures of activities.

69. *Finding Missing Parts.* The teacher may use pictures from old readers, textbooks, magazines, and newspapers. Parts of the pictures are cut off, and the children have to find the missing parts, among another group of pictures. For example, cut off the fenders from a picture of a car, or the tail from a picture of a horse. This activity is not recommended for extremely anxious children.

70. *What Could It Be?* The teacher draws a circle on the chalkboard and says, "What is this?" If a child answers "A circle," the teacher replies, "Good! Now, look at this." She draws an identical circle next to the first one, and says, "If it isn't a circle, what could it be?" Some one will say "A ball." "Good!" says the teacher. She adds a few details to the second circle to make it look like a baseball, then draws a third circle. "If it isn't a circle and it isn't a ball, what could it be?" The game is continued for six or eight circle pictures; then the children are asked to copy the pictures and put them together in one scene. For younger children, this can be done at the chalkboard with hints and help from the teacher.

   On another day the same game can be played with other shapes such as triangles, squares, rectangles, ovals, and irregular shapes. After much experience, children can be asked to combine shapes in their drawings.

71. *Paper People.* Commercial paper dolls can be used, or paper people (men, women, children) may be made out of tagboard by teacher and/or child. Clothes are made for the people for all seasons of the year and for all kinds of activities (sports, dancing, sleeping, etc.). Children are to dress the people appropriately for the season and activity presented. Ideas for clothing can be found in magazines and mail-order catalogs.

24

A variation on this activity is to scramble all the clothes and have children match the correct clothes to the person by size, activity, sex, or season.

72. *Squiggles.* The teacher draws a random squiggly line on the chalkboard, and the child must make a picture out of it. When all the children have understood the game, it can be played with paper and pencil by a group. Each child makes a squiggle and passes it to the next child, the last child giving his to the first.

    A variation is to specify what must be found in a squiggle (e.g., a man's face, an animal, a flower, a car).

EYE-HAND COORDINATION

Eye-hand exercises reinforce visual comparison skills.

Bi-manual Straight Lines

Clock Hands.[9] The teacher draws a large circle on the chalkboard, using full arm movements, and marks it off in a clock pattern. The child fixes his gaze on the center of the circle and, with a piece of chalk in each hand, simultaneously draws straight lines connecting specified positions, in the sequences shown below.

    Each combination of positions should be practiced in different directions (in to the midpoint and out from the midpoint) several times on each occasion; but do *not* change the combination of positions within any practice session until the child is very familiar with a combination and quite adept at it. A child could become very confused and build up a negative reaction to this kind of exercise, which is otherwise often regarded by children as a funny stunt.

73. *Horizontal lines*:

LEFT HAND	RIGHT HAND
9 to center	— 3 to center
center to 9	— center to 3
9 to center	— center to 3
center to 9	— 3 to center

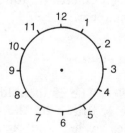

(*continued*)

[9] Adapted from Getman, *How to Develop Your Child's Intelligence.*

74. *Vertical lines*:

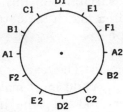

    LEFT HAND   RIGHT HAND

       6 to center — 12 to center

       center to 6 — center to 12

       6 to center — center to 12

       center to 6 — 12 to center

       Follow the same routines but reversing hands (left—12 to center, etc.).

75. *Diagonals.* Follow similar routines using 1 and 7, 2 and 8, etc.

76. *Varied combinations.* Follow similar routines combining horizontal and vertical, horizontal and diagonal, and vertical and diagonal movements. Examples:

    LEFT HAND   RIGHT HAND

       9 to center — 12 to center

       center to 11 — 3 to center

       10 to center — center to 6

Following Dots

77. The teacher places a dot on the chalkboard. The child puts his chalk on it. The teacher makes another dot, and the child connects his dot to this with a straight line. The teacher then moves to make other dots, and the child follows with his chalk. Emphasize quick, full arm movements. After a little practice, work up to various shapes. Later, have the child reproduce these shapes.

78. Use commercial "follow-the-dots" books, or the exercises in many newspapers.

Bi-manual Figures[10]

79. *Circles.* The child holds a piece of chalk in each hand. He looks at a large X drawn on the chalkboard. With both hands at once, he draws circles at left and right of the X, using full arm movements, in the sequence shown:

---

[10] *Ibid.*

Circles going out from the midpoint.

Circles going in toward the midpoint.

Both hands going clockwise.

Both hands going counter-clockwise.

80. *Other Figures.* Do routines similar to those described in § 79, substituting triangles, squares, rectangles, and diamonds for the circles.

Coloring

Coloring in Stencils[11]

81. At each stage of this activity, the child is to color a 4-inch square. The teacher should make sure the entire square is filled in.
  A. The first stencil, made of heavy cardboard, is a 6-inch square with a 4-inch square cut out of the center, leaving a 1-inch frame. The child colors within the frame.
  B. The square frame has one side removed. Substitute a heavy black line for the missing side. Have the child color within the square.
  C. Remove the top strip, making an L-shaped stencil, substituting heavy lines for the missing strips.
  D. Remove the bottom strip, leaving only the strip along the left side, using heavy lines to finish the square.

Coloring Other Things

82. Use simple forms outlined in heavy black lines: square, circle, triangle, rectangle, etc. Starting with a square, just following the stencil coloring activity, will provide continuity.

83. Use regular coloring books. Be sure the child understands the various parts of the picture he is to color, so that he does not, for example, color

---

[11] Adapted from *A Teaching Method for Brain-Injured and Hyperactive Children*, edited by William M. Cruickshank *et al.* Copyright © 1961 by Syracuse University Press, Syracuse, N.Y. All rights reserved. Used by permission of the publisher.

one sleeve of a shirt blue and the rest of the shirt red, caught up in the separation of the sleeve detail, and adding to his own confusion with the resulting colored picture. The teacher can prevent this kind of dissociation by outlining the separate elements in the picture with the color the child is to use in that part of the picture.

Cutting[12]

Using scissors combines small-motor activity with eye-hand coordination activity.

84. Have the child do these cutting exercises in sequence:
    A. Cut on a heavy straight line between two pieces of cardboard glued or stapled to the paper. The cardboard serves to guide the scissors.
    B. Cut on a heavy straight line using one piece of cardboard as a guide.
    C. Cut on a heavy straight line using no cardboard guide.
    D. Cut out geometric figures made with heavy straight (not curved) lines. Change colors with change of direction.
    E. Cut heavy curved lines and circles.
    F. Cut out simple pictures outlined with heavy black lines.
    G. Cut out more complex pictures and mount them on cardboard. This also helps establish foreground-background perception.

Sequencing Patterns

85. *Straws and Squares.* Squares of colored paper about one inch square are alternated with one-inch lengths of paper drinking straws to make sequences. The children are required to string squares and straws in a particular sequence, using blunt needle and thread. Shoelaces can be substituted for the needle and thread for younger children, if holes are punched in the squares first. Simple *paper-straw/paper-straw* patterns can be varied by requiring color variations, or by *paper-straw-straw/paper-straw-straw* kinds of patterns. Children can also create their own patterns for other children to copy.

Drawing

Easy Stages[13]

86. Have the child draw by following dotted lines in geometric figures and patterns, then color in the resulting form. Use simple patterns.

---

[12] *Ibid.*

[13] *Ibid.*

87. Have the child copy a drawing in a step-by-step fashion.

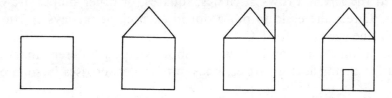

Graph Paper Pictures

88. Simple line drawings can be copied, reduced, or enlarged by making a square grid over the original and then copying, square by square, on graph paper with squares the same size or smaller or larger than those of the grid.

Action Pictures

89. *Five-Dot People.*[14] Make five dots far apart on a page (or on the chalkboard). First the teacher demonstrates, as follows: Select one dot as the head, and draw a circle around it. Then draw hands on two others and feet on two others. Then, using a straight line for the body and V-shaped lines for the arms and legs, connect the dots to make an action picture. Other pictures are then made by individual children or groups of children.

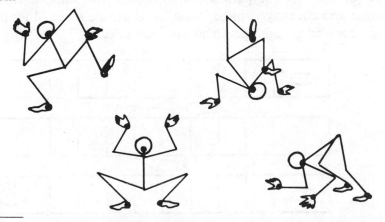

---

[14] Adapted from *Art Today and Every Day: Classroom Activities for the Elementary School Year,* by Jenean Romberg and Miriam Rutz. Copyright © 1972 by Parker Publishing Company, Inc., West Nyack, N.Y. 10994. All rights reserved. Used by permission of the publisher.

Left to Right

90. *Dots in Circles.* Give the child a sheet of paper that has a green margin line at the left and rows of circles, squares, or other shapes drawn at the right. Direct the child to put a dot in each circle, always starting at the green line (green is for GO).

Variation: With rows of two or more shapes, different marks can be made in them (dots in circles, lines in triangles, crosses in squares, etc.).

green margin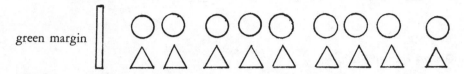

91. *Lines in Lines.* This is a variation of the Dots in Circles game. At the right of the green margin line are rows of vertical lines arranged in groups of varying number. Starting from the green line, the child is to draw a horizontal line through each cluster of vertical lines, making sure the horizontal line does not extend beyond the outside vertical lines.

green margin

92. *Mouse and Cheese.* Give the child a piece of paper divided into rows of boxes and tell him to mark the path the mouse must take to get to the cheese. He must mark every box in every row, always starting at the *big* box (at the left); the path could be drawn with lines, dots, or X's. For mouse and cheese you might want to substitute some other combination (e.g., car and garage, child and birthday cake).

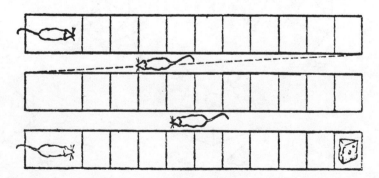

[15] Adapted from *Reading Aids Through the Grades* (2nd rev. ed.), by David H. Russell, Etta E. Karp, and Anne Marie Mueser (New York: Teachers College Press, 1975), pp. 88-90, 61. Used by permission.

93. *Letter Game.* Prepare sheets with short rows of lower-case and capital letters variously grouped and arranged. Have the child draw a line through (or a circle around) the big letters (or the small letters).

AAaa   aaaA   AAAa   aaAA

CCC   Ccc   ccC   CCcc   ccc   CCC   cCCC

B B B B   bbBBBB   b b b b   BbBbb

D d DDD   D ddd   DDd   D D D dd d d

SSS S s s s sSS   SS   s s s   SS Ss sS

Visual Tracking

94. Select a passage from a reader at the child's level or below. The child is instructed to cross out the letters of the alphabet in order as they occur in the passage. (Cross out the first *a*, then the first *b* after that, and so forth.) The teacher can have a marked copy of the passage to use for a check sheet. Example:[16]

The lady took Max by the hand. "I can help you," she said.
Together they looked for the zookeeper. They found him standing in front of the cafeteria.
"This young man just lost his mother," said the lady.
The zookeeper smiled. "I'm the best mother-finder in the country," he said. "I can help you."
"Goodbye," said the lady. "I have to go quickly now. I promised to meet my grandson at the lion house at three o'clock, and I'm late." She waved her hand and hurried away.
"Well," said the zookeeper, "Whose little boy are you?"
"Mommy's," said Max.
"Okay," said the zookeeper, "Let's find her then."

---

[16] Betty Van Witsen, *Whose Little Boy Are You?* (New York: Avon Books, 1953).

31

Secret Code

95. Together the class can devise a picture code for the alphabet, and encode and decode secret messages to each other. The teacher can prepare messages for the class on the board or on ditto for practice at first. Here is a sample code in which each item is a very simple picture for a word that begins with the actual letter the picture represents.

Finger Numbers

96. *"Show Me."* Call out a number to primary age children and have them show a finger configuration they can use in calculating. For example, the teacher says, "Show me four." The children must show 4 fingers, thumb tucked in. "Show me eight." Children show 4 on each hand, both thumbs tucked in. "Show me five." Children show one hand. "Show me six." Children show one hand and the thumb of the other hand. Later, when all the children are proficient at showing taught configurations, alternate ones can be shown—for example, 8 as a 5-and-3 pattern rather than 4-and-4. Following are commonly used patterns for calculating:

    1–thumb of dominant hand
    2–thumb and index finger of dominant hand
    3–thumb, index finger, and middle finger of dominant hand
    4–four fingers, thumb tucked in, of dominant hand
    5–dominant hand
    6–dominant hand and thumb of other hand
    7–dominant hand and thumb and index finger of other hand
    8–four fingers of both hands, thumbs tucked in
    9–dominant hand and four fingers of other hand
    10–both hands

Popular Pastimes

97. A variety of activities that foster skillful eye-hand relationships:

Ball catching. (Begin with large ball at first, later reduce the size.)

Ball throwing and catching (against a wall).

Block building.

Dart games.

Folding paper or napkins. Simple origami (Japanese paper folding) is excellent practice for eye-hand coordination, and is greatly enjoyed by most children. Some sample paper-folding activities are described in the Appendix, and books on origami are commercially available.

Jacks.

Marbles.

Modeling clay or salt dough.

Nail pounding.

Cooking: measuring, peeling fruit, buttering bread, pouring, etc.

Pick-up-sticks.

Sewing: sewing cards and more advanced sewing.

Knitting: with regular knitting needles and with horse-rein sets.

Soap carving.

Shoelace tying.

Typing.

Writing.

Painting. For very young children (under 4 years old), large outdoor paintbrushes and a bucket of water, used to paint the blackboard, or used outdoors to paint a wall. For older children, easel painting with tempera paints.

Peg board activities. There are many commercial variations on the simple peg board.

Construction toys such as Rig-a-Jig, Tinker Toys, Lincoln Logs, and Block City.

98. *Finger Trace.* The teacher draws a shape or writes a word on the chalkboard. The child dips his fingers in water and traces the shape.

99. *Sponge Writing.* Children can practice writing on the chalkboard with sponges dipped in water and then partially wrung out so that there will not be too much dripping. In a more precise version of this, requiring a pencil grip, children can use stamp moisteners, which are small cylindrical plastic containers with sponge tips. (The cylinder is filled with water, and there is less dripping than with plain sponges.)

5
Auditory Perception and Language Skills

Many of the activities described in this chapter involve reading, spelling, and writing skills as well as auditory perception or imagery. It is well to keep in mind that children's language competence is usually highly developed—through listening and speaking—long before they start to learn to read, and that subsequent language experience continues to be based on auditory imagery: the "written word" is not the word; it is a symbol for the (heard and spoken) word.

LISTENING GAMES

Familiar Sounds

100. *"Talking Drum."* The teacher beats the drum to the rhythm of a child's name; for example: "Helen Johnson" (DAH da DAH da), "Emmanuel Robertson" (da DAH da da DAH da da). Initially the teacher should say the name while sounding the drumbeats, later just mouth it silently. The child holds his hand up when his name is sounded on the drum. He uses the visual clue of reading the teacher's lips. When the children become adept at this game, the teacher can drop the visual clue. Later, the children's motor activity is used to reinforce their auditory perception. They can beat out one another's names—or other words, such as new words from the reading vocabulary list, or particular holiday words such as "Thanksgiving" (DAH DAH da) and "Santa Claus" (DAH da da). Or, the children can guess words the teacher beats out. For example, the teacher says "See if you can guess what word the drum is saying. The word is something about Thanksgiving." She beats out "DAH da." The children must guess a word of the DAH-da rhythm having to do with the Thanksgiving holiday, such as "dinner," "pumpkin," "turkey," or "stuffing." Such words as "holiday," "company," or "mashed potatoes" would be counted wrong.

101. The teacher taps a pencil on the desk and proceeds as in §100.

102. The teacher bounces a ball. The children close their eyes. When called on, the child must tell how many times the ball bounced. Do it only one, two, or three times at first. If the child cannot count, he may imitate the movement the correct number or times.

103. Show the children two objects, for example a cup and spoon. Have them close their eyes. Stir the spoon in the cup, and then call on a child to tell what you did. Tap the cup and repeat the process. Then show other objects and make sounds with them: a pencil and ruler (tapping, scraping, rolling); a book and a card (riffling the pages, patting, rubbing); and so on. In this exercise the child sees the objects but has to identify what is done with them by sound alone.

104. "*What Is It?*" The children close their eyes. The teacher makes a familiar sound and calls on a child to identify it. In this exercise, the children do not see the object; their only clue is sound. If the children cannot keep their eyes closed, the teacher can perform the action behind a screen. Later, one child may make a sound while the others, including the teacher, close their eyes and guess. Vary this game with the production of two sounds, and ask if they are the same or different, and then identify them. These are some sounds the teacher might make:

tearing paper	bouncing a ball
sharpening a pencil	rattling a rattle
walking, running, shuffling feet	snapping the lights on
clapping hands	knocking on a door
sneezing, coughing	blowing a pitch pipe
tapping (on glass, wood, metal)	dropping an object
jingling money	moving a desk or chair
opening a window	snapping fingers
pouring water	blowing nose
shuffling cards	opening or closing drawers
blowing a whistle	stirring paint in a jar
banging blocks	clearing the throat
ringing a bell	splashing water
vibrating sound (bobby pin)	rubbing sandpaper together
sweeping sound (brush, broom)	chattering teeth
raising or lowering window shades	closing a pocketbook
beating erasers	clicking the tongue
leafing through pages in a book	crumpling paper
cutting with scissors	writing on the blackboard
shaking paper clips in a glass	opening a box

breaking a piece of chalk	sighing
rattling keys	striking a match
snapping rubber bands	rubbing palms together

105. "*What Do You Hear?*" The purpose of this game is to help the children focus their attention on sounds rather than to test whether they can identify them, so the teacher should try to use sounds that can be heard clearly and are easily identified. Begin the activity by calling the children's attention to environmental sounds and naming them. Later the teacher says, "Let's all sit quietly, as quietly as we can. What different sounds can we hear?" (Car passing by, voice of the teacher in the next room, clock ticking, footsteps, dog barking, car horns, etc.)

106. "*Near or Far?*" Identify outdoor sounds with eyes closed and tell if they are near or far.

107. "*High or Low?*"[17] Direct the children's attention to the pitch of sounds when they listen to a note struck on the piano, guitar, autoharp, or xylophone. Then strike a note an octave above the first note. Repeat several times. When the high note is being struck, ask the children to stand with their arms high above their heads; when the low note is struck, ask them to squat low. Extend this activity later to "higher," "lower," "the same." Use a small staircase and let the children go up and down, according to the pitch of the music.

108. "*Loud or Soft?*"[18] Identify loud and soft sounds, and play games like those in §107. Develop prediction of loudness or softness from the appearance of the object; for example: big and little bells, ruler and toothpick, pot cover and key.

Animal Sounds and Other Sound Effects

109. The teacher makes an animal sound and the children identify the animal. Later, the children form two teams. A member of Team A makes an animal sound, and a member of Team B must identify it. The procedure is then reversed.

110. The children are assigned particular animals to imitate. This can be varied and made more interesting if the teacher requires a particular quality in the sound. For example: "You are a mother cat calling her baby in to dinner." "You are a boy bee having a fight with his brother." The teacher should try to have the children imitate the actual sounds,

---

[17] Adapted by permission from *Growing into Reading*, by Marion Monroe (p. 119). Copyright 1951 by Scott, Foresman and Company. Reprinted by permission.
[18] *Ibid.*, pp. 118-119.

rather than use conventional words for them ("bow-wow," "meow," etc.). Children also enjoy making the animal sounds in songs like "Old MacDonald Had a Farm" and "I Had a Cat."

111. *Nonvocal Sound Effects.*[19] Let the children try producing such sound effects as rain (drumming fingers), wind (blowing through a tube), galloping horses (tapping sticks on a box or banging coconut shells together), ocean waves (letting sand slide back and forth in a box), fire burning (crackling cellophane). The teacher can tell or read a story, and the children can supply the sound effects.

112. *Timbre.*[20] One child sits behind a screen and shakes a rattle, turns an egg beater, sweeps with a broom, claps his hands, uses a pencil sharpener, crushes a piece of paper, pours water from a bottle into a glass, pops a balloon, blows a whistle, toots a horn, saws a piece of wood, hammers a nail, rings a bell, and so on. The other children guess the activity from its sound, and may try to imitate it vocally or describe it.

In referring to these sounds—and others that occur in the course of the day—take advantage of opportunities to use descriptive words such as *whir, swish, rattle, crash, bang, click, buzz, squeak, murmur, slosh, rumble, toot, snort, hiss, gurgle,* etc.

Rhythms and Repetitions

113. *Story Sounds.* The children repeat refrains as the teacher reads a story. Good stories to use with younger children are: "The Little Red Hen," "Chicken Little," "The Gingerbread Man," "Millions of Cats" (by Wanda Gag), "The Musicians of Bremen," and "Ask Mr. Bear" (by Marjorie Flack).

114. *Drumbeats.* The children imitate by clapping. The teacher should begin with simple, even strokes on the drum (one, two, or three), and then progress to simple rhythms accented on the first beat (2/4, 4/4, 3/4), then to more complicated rhythms including some slow and some fast beats.

115. *Counting Out.* Nonsense counting-out rhymes require imitation, aid the child's sense of rhythm, and give practice in articulation. Some rhymes that children like are:

---

[19] *Ibid.,* p. 121.
[20] *Ibid.,* p. 120.

Wing wong way
Tisha lumma say
Lumma see lumma so
Tisha Lumma sinky mo

Sinky mo to taffy
Taffy to koko
Wing wong way
Tisha lumma lumma say.

Ibbety bibbety sibbety sab
Ibbety bibbety canal boat
Up the ferry
Down the ferry
Out goes Y-O-U.

116. "*Cookie Jar*." The children chant rhythmically, following the teacher's lead:

> *Teacher:* Who stole the cookie from the cookie jar?
> *Children:* Jane stole the cookie from the cookie jar!
> *Jane:* Who, me?
> *Children:* Yes, you!
> *Jane:* Couldn't be!
> *Children:* Then who?
> *Jane:* Billy stole the cookie from the cookie jar!
> *Billy:* Who, me?
> *(And so on.)*

Following Directions

117. *Do As You're Told.* Give simple directions, such as "Come to my desk," "Open the door," and "Look up." Increase complexity by giving two sequential directions, and then by indicating the manner in which the direction must be carried out ("Walk to the door noisily and come back quietly.").

118. *Come When You're Called.* This game can be played at line-up time (for lunch or dismissal) or just for its own sake. The teacher calls children to the front of the room by descriptions of what they're wearing, by initials of their names, or by other descriptive means. Groups as well as individuals can be called this way. For example: "All children wearing blue." "All girls who have an *R* in their name."

119. "*You Must*."[21] This game is a variation of "Simon Says." The children form a circle around a leader who gives directions, some of which are prefaced with "You must." The children are to follow only the "you must" directions, ignoring any that do not begin with "you must." Directions to be used may include walking forward, hopping on one foot, bending forward, standing tall, and so forth.

This game can be varied by having the children follow the directions when the leader says "do this" and not when he says "do that." Play only one version of this game on a single day. Too much variety will confuse the children.

120. "*Giants*." The children form a circle. The leader stands in the center. When he calls "Giants" the children stand on tip-toe. When he calls "Men" they stand naturally, but very straight. When he calls "Dwarfs" they stoop. Change leaders often.

121. "*Bring Me*." The teacher tells the group to listen very carefully. He then says that he will call a child's name, and say "Bring me." When he says bring me something that can be brought, the child must bring it. But when he says something silly, like "Bring me the window" or "Bring me your house" the child must stay quietly in his chair without moving. This game is helpful in teaching children to control impulsive responses.

122. "*Fruit Salad*." Children take the names of different fruits. The leader calls out the names of two fruits. The children who have taken those names must change places. Every now and then, the leader calls out "Fruit Salad" and everyone changes places.

This game can be varied by having the children take the names of animals and calling the game *Zoo*, or the names of flowers and calling the game *Garden*, or the names of different foods and calling the game *Restaurant* (or *Macdonalds*?); or by using any other category that appeals to the children and will hold their attention.

123. "*Listen Carefully*." To give practice in following simple directions, each child is equipped with a blank sheet of paper and crayons. The teacher says "Listen carefully and do exactly what I say." He then gives three or four simple directions such as:

Draw a line near the top of your page.
Draw a blue flower near the middle of your page.
Take the black crayon. Draw a ball near the bottom of your page.

---

[21] From *Listening Aids Through the Grades*, by David H. Russell and Elizabeth F. Russell (New York: Teachers College Press, 1959), p. 20. Used by permission.

In the beginning the teacher should give only one direction at a time. Later this can be increased to two, three, or four.

The children can also be given pages with a few simple objects drawn on them, and the directions can be more exacting:

Join the two men with a red line.

Put a circle around the cat and draw a line under the tree.

Cross out the picture of the ball, draw a line under the flower, and put a circle under the moon.

Draw a line from the horse to the boy, cross out the star, and put a line over the cup.

The children are not to follow a direction until the teacher is through speaking. He may say "Go!" as a signal.

124. *Giant Steps.* (Another name for this game is "*May I?*") The leader stands at one end of the room facing a group of children. The leader tells each child in turn what kind of forward steps to take—for example, "Joey, you may take three giant steps." Joey then must reply, "May I?" The leader then answers either "Yes, you may" or "No, you may not; you may take four baby steps" or some other direction. Again the child must say "May I?" and the leader must respond. The object of the game is to reach the leader, tag him, and run back to starting position without the leader catching you. The player who succeeds becomes the next leader. If a child forgets to say "May I?" he must go all the way back to the starting position. Players may sneak forward, but if they are caught moving without permission they are sent back to starting position. The different kinds of steps are *giant steps* (a step as long as a child can stretch), *baby steps* (one foot placed in front of the other, heel touching toe), *lady steps* (medium-sized steps), *banana peels* (sliding one foot forward as though slipping on a banana peel, and landing on the furthest forward spot) and *umbrella steps* (one foot forward, spinning on that foot, then placing the other foot as far forward as possible without losing balance.)

125. "*Tornado.*" One child is selected to be the weather man. He calls out which way the wind is blowing—from the front, the back, the left, or the right. When he calls the direction, all the players must face that way. When he calls "Tornado!" everyone spins around and lands facing front.

126. "*This Is My Ear.*" One child points to any part of his body (except his ear) and says, "This is my ear." He then names another child. The child who is named must point to his ear and say, "This is my _____" naming the part of the body the first child pointed to. He then points to another part of his body, calls it by the wrong name and calls on another child.

41

AUDITORY MEMORY

In addition to those presented here, many other activities in this book provide practice in auditory memory. (They include, for example, §§113, 117, 123, 141, 147, 149, 159, 162, 164, and 170.) And of course any memorizing and repeating of something listened to (a drum rhythm, a melody, a poem, the words of a song) is an exercise in auditory memory.

127. *Restaurant.*[22] Have the children cut out from magazines colored pictures of bread, pies, cakes, fruits, vegetables, and meat dishes. These are placed on a table over which a "cook" presides. Three or four children—the "customers"—sit around another small table, which may be set with paper plates, knives, forks, and spoons that have been designed, cut out, and colored by members of the class. Before taking their seats, the customers look over the cook's display. The "waiter" takes each customer's order and repeats the order to the cook. The cook places the appropriate pictures on a tray, which the waiter carries back to the table. The waiter then distributes each "dish" to the proper customer.

Similar games can be played dealing with various kinds of things (clothing, toys, garden supplies, furniture) processed by various agents (salesman, manager, stock clerk) in different places (store window, store, delivery truck).

128. *Go Together.* The teacher names an activity or place that is familiar to the children, and they take turns naming things that go with the activity, each child repeating the entire list. For example: *a trip to the park* (swings, grass, slide, fountain, trees, seesaw); *a day at the beach* (sand, ocean, sandwiches, bathing suit, beach ball, pail and shovel); *the library* (books, librarian's desk, card file, display cases, tables, carrels, Xerox machine); *the lunchroom* (tables, garbage cans, lunches, steam table, cash register, benches, pictures); *drugstore* (prescription counter, cashier, book display, toiletries, toothpaste).

LANGUAGE SOUNDS

Rhyming and Differentiation

129. *Oral Rhyming.* The teacher says several jingles, using the children's names as rhyme words. Examples:

Mark, Mark,	Mike, Mike,	Ellen, Ellen,
Went to the park.	Rode his bike.	Ate a melon.

---

[22] Adapted from Monroe, *Growing into Reading*, p. 183. Used by permission of the publisher.

He then supplies the first line of another jingle, and the beginning of its next line, and calls on a child to supply the rhyming word.

When the children are thoroughly familiar with the various rhymes on their own names, they can supply the rhymes for one another's names, and then rhymes for other words can be introduced, using the same rhythm.

130. *"Wrong Word."* The teacher says a group of three words, two of which rhyme and one which does not. Example:

tell, honk, sell
man, can, toy
ride, hall, ball

A child is called on to say the rhyming words and omit the "wrong word." Some children will need to hear a series of four or five rhyming words instead of just two, but later the number can be reduced.

131. *Nursery Rhymes and Jingles.* Edward Lear's *Nonsense Alphabets* are funny and full of rhyming sounds. Be sure that the jingles and poems that you select for this activity are accurate in their rhymes, as some Mother Goose poems are not. "Jack and Jill," for example, rhymes *water* with *after*; "One, two, Buckle My Shoe" rhymes *fourteen* with *courting*.

One way to use these is for the teacher to read aloud two or more rhyming lines, stopping before the end of the last line to let children guess the rhyme word.

132. *Word Families.* The teacher draws two houses on the blackboard. In one house the ALL family lives. In the other house the IN family lives. The children suggest the names of words living in each family house and the teacher writes them in the windows of the house. For variety, the teacher can say a word, and call on a child to tell in which house it belongs.

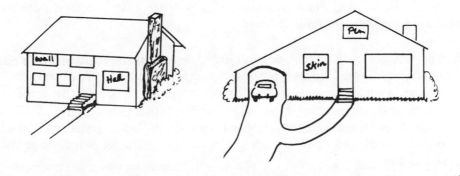

133. *Rhyme Game.* The teacher says (for example): "I'm thinking of something you sleep in that rhymes with *red*." "I'm thinking of something you wear on your foot that rhymes with *two*." Later, leave out the clues and say simply, "I'm thinking of something that rhymes with _____." The children guess individually. Any correct rhyme is counted as correct at first. When the children are really adept at this game, only the actual word the teacher is thinking of is considered correct, although all good rhymes are praised. Caution: Be sure the words rhyme accurately. *Ann* does not rhyme with *sand*. These small differences must be pointed out to help the children listen all the way through to the end of the word.

134. "*Same or Different.*" The teacher pronounces a word, then pronounces the same word or one that is very slightly different from it. The child called on must say whether they are the "same" or "different." Here are a *few* examples of the virtually infinite supply of slightly *different* pairs:

bag–back	dug–duck	oil–earl
bang–bank	eat–heat	rode–wrote
beg–bag	feel–fill	singing–sinking
boat–both	fell–felt	shoe–chew
chip–ship	less–lets	sleep–slip
day–they	necks–next	tin–thin

Initial Consonant Sounds

Note: It is important to structure initial consonant games quite differently from rhyme games, so there is no confusion between them. It is advisable to avoid the use of pictures in rhyme games, and to use them extensively in initial consonant games, to emphasize the difference between the word aspects being considered.

It is also important, of course, not to confuse sounds with letters. For example, the words *phone* and *pony* begin with different consonant sounds, as do *tub* and *thumb*; and the words *can* and *keg* begin with the same consonant sound, as do *jelly/germ* and *city/sun*.

135. The teacher shows pictures of objects whose names begin with the same consonant sound (*popcorn, pony, pumpkin, puppy*). The pictures are named, and the teacher points out that the words begin the same way. When two or three initial sounds are developed ("p", "t", and "k" are good ones for the beginning, since they look different on the mouth when pronounced), the children can play games organizing words in terms of initial sounds.

136. The teacher divides the chalkboard into three sections and puts a picture of something beginning with a "p" sound on the chalk ledge under the first section, something beginning with a "t" sound under the second section, and something beginning with a "k" sound under the third section. The children are called, one at a time, to take a card from a pack of picture cards, say the name of the pictured item, and place the card where it belongs. When more initial sounds have been developed, such card games as Rummy or Go Fish can be played with picture cards, easily made by pasting onto tagboard pictures cut from old phonics and reading workbooks, magazines, and so on.

137. *Shopping.* The leader says, "I went to the supermarket and I bought lettuce." The next player must go to the supermarket and buy something else beginning with the same consonant sound.

In a variation on this game, players can "shop" in a different kind of store.

Another variation, more difficult, is to have each child change the kind of store. For example: *Child 1*—"I went to the supermarket and I bought pears." *Child 2*—"I went to the hardware store and I bought pliers." *Child 3*—"I went to the flower store and I bought petunias."

Final Consonant Sounds

138. The teacher pronounces several words that have the same final consonant sound (*make, look, work, pick*). It is a good idea to avoid rhyming words and words with the same initial consonant, in order to focus the child's attention on the final sound. The childen are asked to clap when they hear another word that ends the same way (e.g., *park*). The teacher then says a series of words, some ending with the "k" sound, some ending with other sounds. Sometimes the sound must be exaggerated in pronunciation at the beginning of this activity, but later, in connected speech, the sounds should of course be spoken naturally.

Locating Consonant Sounds

139. *Beginning, Middle, or End?* The teacher says (making the sound, *not* naming the letter), "Listen for the "t" sound. Is it at the beginning, middle, or end?" He gives examples of "t" sounds in initial (*top, tell,*

Tom), medial (*letter, between, writing*), and final (*bat, coat, light*) positions. The teacher then says a list of words containing "t" sounds, and the children take turns locating the positions of the letters. Do the same with other consonants.

140. *Hitching Post Game.*[23] The game in § 139 can be given dramatic structure by telling the children to pretend they are cowboys, and that they must hitch their ponies to the right hitching post. Three vertical lines, representing the initial, medial, and final positions, are drawn on the chalkboard. The teacher says words containing consonant sounds in these three positions. The "cowboy" whose turn it is "hitches" the sound to the correct "post" (either by writing the letter, if he knows it, next to the appropriate vertical line, or by making a mark on the line).

Later, the children can work on individual sheets of paper, write numbers 1 to 10, draw three "hitching posts" next to each number, and circle the correct one for each word as it is read by the teacher or by another child. This is difficult for some children, since they must take a temporal sequence and translate it into a set of spatially organized symbols. These children may need some initial practice in this aspect of the game.

SEQUENCE

Conceptual Sequence

141. *Story Cut-ups.* A simple story, well within or below the children's reading level (to ensure focus on the sequence aspect of the activity and not on the reading skill) is cut up into parts and pasted on pieces of tagboard. The teacher tells the story. The teacher then mixes up the different parts of the story and hands them out to the children. The child who thinks he has the first part of the story reads it. The others follow until the whole story is read.

This activity must be kept very simple at first. Sometimes it is necessary to begin with a familiar poem that the children all know by heart, rather than a story, then take up stories cut into one-sentence pieces, the whole story consisting of the same number of sentences as there are children participating in the activity, and finally progress to more complicated stories.

142. *All Day Long.* The teacher begins this game by telling what she did at a particular time of day, and then calling on children in turn to tell what they did at that time of day. For example, the teacher might say, "After lunch yesterday, I played ball." When the children have become familiar

---

[23] Russell and Russell, *Listening Aids* . . . , p. 41. Used by permission.

46

with recalling different times of the day, the game can progress to having the children follow the sequence of an entire day's activities, each one telling something that happens next.

For example: Child 1: *When I got out of bed I turned off the alarm clock.* Child 2: *I went to the bathroom.* Child 3: *I got dressed.* Child 4: *I ate breakfast.* Child 5: *I fed my goldfish.* Child 6: *I went to school.* And so forth.

143. *Continued Stories.* The teacher or one child begins a story (based on a picture if the children have difficulty getting started). At a high point, another child is asked to continue the story for a couple of sentences. Then a third child picks it up, and so forth.

144. *Scrambled Sentences.* Simple sentences are cut into three or four parts to be reassembled correctly by the children in turn. Begin with sentences like "I went to the store" (cut up into *I went / to / the store"*) or "It is time for lunch" (*It is / time / for lunch*). Progress to more difficult sentences like "Susan ran down the street with her doll carriage" (*Susan ran / down the street / with / her doll carriage*) or "My mother will call for me if it rains" (*My mother / will call / for me / if / it rains*). The children must read the resulting reassembled sentences aloud to hear if they make sense. The final step in this activity is scrambling *all* the words in a sentence. Begin with very simple declarative sentences such as "You are my friend" and progress to more difficult ones like "Where do the birds go when the weather gets cold?"

Rote-Learned Sequence

145. *What Went Wrong?* The teacher uses a rote-learned sequence with which the children are familiar (days of the week, months of the year, letters of the alphabet, numbers one to ten, etc.). The teacher says the words with one of them in the wrong place. The children raise their hands when they hear a word out of sequence and correct it. This can be varied by using poems and jingles that the children are familiar with, instead of single words, and saying a line out of sequence, such as "Baa, baa black sheep, three bags full." This activity is very funny to most children, and they enjoy correcting the teacher.

146. *Missing Words.*[24] Give the first and last words with which a well-known jingle begins and ends. Let the children think of the words between; e.g.: "Jack . . . nimble," "Old . . . Hubbard," "Mary . . . lamb."

Later, let the children supply the first and last words and other children supply the missing words.

---

[24] Monroe, *Growing into Reading,* p. 183. Used by permission of the publisher.

47

147. *Make Sense*. The teacher says: "Listen. *I have a car*. Does that make sense? Yes, it does. Listen. *Car a have I*. Does that make sense? No, it doesn't. *Car a have I*. Billy, make sense. Fix the sentence to make sense." If Billy cannot do it, the teacher demonstrates with the correct sequence of words. Scrambled sentences are then presented to the other children, who are asked to "Make sense." Initially, all sentences (before scrambling) must have simple patterns and be confined to three or four words, with no ambiguity in meaning. Examples:

Give me the game.	She is a girl.
They sang a song.	Mother told me.
He reads a book.	We will eat lunch.
You can play ball.	He was sleepy.

When the children are proficient at this, sentences can have more words and slightly more complex structures. Examples:

She went to the store.	She sat on the bench.
They argued with him.	He laughed at the clown.
We thought of a plan.	I hope he will not go.

Gradually increase the length and complexity of sentences. Let the children scramble sentences for each other if they want to.

148. *Telegrams*. A fairly long word is printed on the chalkboard; for example, *understand*. The players must make up a message, or telegram, using the letters of the word *understand* as the initial letters of the words in the telegram.

EASTERN UNION

UNCLE NED'S DOG EATS ROSES.   SISTER TERRIBLY ANGRY NOW.

DONALD

149. *Sentence Stretch*. The teacher (or one child) begins a sentence by saying any word that could begin a sentence (i.e., not words like "and" or "but"). The second player adds a word, without repeating the first word. The third child adds another word, and so forth. The object of the game is not to let a sentence end on you. If it does, you have a point against you. The winner of the game is the person with the fewest points. No two-word sentences are allowed (such as "I can" or "They are.")

Example: Player 1: *Every*. Player 2: *girl*. Player 3: *in*. Player 4: *the*. Player 5: *world*. Player 6: *wants*. Player 7: *to*. Player 8: *be*. Player 9: *a*. Player 10: *teacher*.

The sentence ended on Player 10, and he gets the point. He could have said "good" instead of "teacher," and avoided the point. Rules can be changed to fit the group of children playing the game, but it is usually necessary to disallow the use of more than three adjectives in sequence or the use of more than one "very" in a sentence.

MEANING DIFFERENTIATION

150. *Homonyms*. Point these out as they come up in the context of activities. Have children dramatize the different uses of the words. Examples:

knot–not	new–knew	piece–peace	there–their
rain–rein–reign	here–hear	write–right	wood–would
ate–eight	for–four	one–won	no–know
break–brake	some–sum	great–grate	die–dye
our–hour	mail–male	to–two–too	week–weak
wait–weight	beat–beet	be–bee	cent–sent–scent
sail–sale	bear–bare	steel–steal	blew–blue
war–wore	so–sew	buy–by	see–sea
heel–heal	flower–flour	threw–through	meet–meat
red–read	him–hymn	sun–son	hole–whole

The children can make up sentences using both homonyms, such as "I sang a hymn for him," or "I can write my name the right way," or "You sew so nicely."

151. *Same Old Cat!* This is a game that uses synonyms. The children sit in a circle. The teacher (or leader) says, "I have a cat that _____" and tells something about the cat's appearance or behavior. The child to her left responds with "I have a cat that _____," using a synonym for the first description. The teacher replies, "Same old cat!" The second player then describes his cat to the next player, and so forth.

Sample sequence: "I have a cat that is golden." "I have a yellow cat." "Same old cat!" "I have a cat that is good." "I have a cat that is bad." "Different cat!" "I have a cat that is naughty." "I have a cat that is bad." "Same old cat!" "I have a cat that's not afraid of dogs." "I have a brave cat." "Same old cat!"

152. *"Double" Words.* These are homographs—words that have two different meanings but are spelled alike and sound alike (e.g., the verb *box* meaning to fist-fight and the noun *box* meaning a container). Words like these lead to confused and concrete thinking. The teacher could start a collection of objects and pictures illustrating both meanings of such words as they come up in context. Many jokes and puns are based on these words as well as on homonyms. Examples:

play	fan	iron	stand
ring	bulb	fork	head
safe	pump	horn	tie
leg	sink	fly	ear
bowl	cap	cool	pipe
punch	shade	bank	letter
run	box	skip	hand
pop	pitch	bill	

153. *Antonyms.* These can be dramatized, and stories can be made up by the children, using antonyms. The teacher can start a story and have individual children supply the missing words. For example:

Once there was a very fat lady who married a man who was not fat at all. He was very _____.

Every morning the lady ate a great big breakfast, but the man did not eat a big breakfast. He ate a _____ breakfast.

One day the lady said to the man, "Let's go and buy a new hat for you." "No" said the man, "I don't want a new hat. I like my _____ one." . . .

Some commonly used antonyms are:

come–go	off–on	then–now
this–that	right–wrong	wide–narrow
all–none	hard–soft	fat–thin
after–before	like–dislike	warm–cool
find–lose	good–bad	laugh–cry

open–close	old–new	near–far
buy–sell	live–die	little–big
start–finish	long–short	yes–no
clean–dirty	small–large	stop–go
funny–sad	pretty–ugly	ask–tell
up–down	right–left	high–low

154. *Synonyms.* Synonyms are more difficult for most children than antonyms. A useful way to teach some of them is through the use of a notebook and pictures. Adjectives and other words describing the picture can be listed in the notebook under each picture. Children can draw pictures for some of the words, and find pictures for others. Here is a list of useful synonyms for young children:

good—nice	near—close	raise—lift	sopping—wet
thin—skinny	rise—go up	jiggle—shake	tired—weary
fast—quickly	carol—song	bad—mean	easy—simple
never—at no time	reply—answer	fat—plump	cold—chilly
almost—nearly	small—tiny	hard—difficult	distant—far
small—little	funny—laughable	solitary—alone	close—shut
old—aged	hurry—rush	allow—permit	cellar—basement
pretty—beautiful	lag—dawdle		

155. *Compound Word Pictures.* Children read rebuses of compound words and then try to make some for other children to guess. Some compound words that lend themselves to this kind of activity are:

firefly	housetop	sawdust	lipstick	eggshell
shoehorn	hatbox	ladybug	sailboat	mailbag
fireman	pineapple	birdhouse	notebook	pancake
horseshoe	armchair	tablespoon	cupcake	cowboy
moonlight	rainbow	fishhook	basketball	

51

These games include creative play with different aspects of language such as the appearance of words as well as meanings and sounds.

156. *"Feathers and Fur."* One child is "It." "It" says "feathers" (or "hair" or "fur" or "skin"). The other children raise their hands and guess the name of an animal that has feathers. One who guesses correctly becomes "It," and names the category for the others to guess from. Probably with very advanced children the number of categories would have to be enlarged to include porcupines and terrapins. This game can lead to interesting use of the encyclopedia.

157. *Word Dominoes.* The purpose of this game is to reinforce the visual image of a written word when the spoken word is heard. It is appropriate only for children with somewhat advanced reading and spelling skills. A category is selected (flowers, cities, foods, boys' names, machines, etc.). The first player gives one word in the category. The next player gives another word in the category that begins with the last letter of the previous word given. For example, in the category of food, the first player might say *apple*; the next, *eggs*; the next, *sugar*; the next, *radish*; the next, *hamburger*; the next, *raspberry jam*; the next, *matzoh*. The words may be written on the blackboard when the game is first played to help the children focus on the last letters of the words.(When place names are used in this game, it is called "Geography.")

158. *Question Words.* Introduce the question words one at a time. Make clear the form in which the answers to questions are to be given. For example, a question beginning with the word "who" requires an answer that tells *which person*; a question beginning with "where" calls for an answer that tells *what place*; a "why" requires an answer beginning with "because" and giving a *reason*; a "how" calls for an answer telling *in what way*; a "when" asks *at what time*. This activity helps the child focus on giving relevant answers to questions rather than giving an answer based on an association with one part of the question, as with the child who, when asked "Where did you go yesterday after school?" replies, "Because my mother took me." The teacher asks a question using one question word. The children reply individually. Later, more than one question word can be used in one question.

159. *Directions and Numbers.* The teacher gives the children paper and pencils, and then gives the following directions:
   A. Listen to this series of numbers and write the third one:
   5–9–4–2–7

B. Listen to this series of numbers and write the next-to-the-last one:
3–7–2–9–8–5
C. Listen to these numbers and write the one that is closest to the number 3.
7–5–0–9–4–6
D. Listen to these numbers and write the largest (or highest).
6–2–7–5–8–4–7
E. Listen to these numbers and write a number less than 10 that is not mentioned.
6–2–8–4–9–7–1

160. *Catching Absurd Details*. Read to the group a paragraph or story in which there is a contradictory or absurd detail. For example: "The room was very cold. The thermometer read over 80." "It was late at night. Everyone was asleep. The sun shone down through the window into Billy's room." "The last time I saw Amy, she had a new hairdo. But the next time I saw her, she changed it back to the way she used to wear it." "It is impossible to get a taxi on a rainy night. Even the empty ones have passengers in them."

161. *What's the Holiday?* The teacher lists on the board, with the times of year in which they occur, the holidays appropriate for the particular group of children, or (with young children) draws or displays pictures associated with the holidays. Then the teacher names various objects and weather conditions, and the children guess the holiday.

162. *"Grandmother's Trunk."* The first player says "I packed my grandmother's trunk with apples" (or anything that begins with the letter *A*). The next player says "I packed my grandmother's trunk with apples and blankets" (repeating the first word and adding a word beginning with *B*). Go through the alphabet. When introducing this game, the teacher may put the alphabet on the chalkboard as a reminder, but later this should be omitted.

163. *Advanced "Grandmother's Trunk."* For children of advanced skills, "Grandmother's Trunk" can be made more difficult (and often hilarious) by observing the following rules: On the *first round*, each player repeats the previous alphabetical sequence of nouns and adds a new noun to it. On the *second round*, each player must preface his new noun with an adjective beginning with the same letter. On the *third round*, a proper noun beginning with the same letter precedes the adjective. On the *fourth round*, another adjective precedes the proper noun. The *fifth round* is like the third, the *sixth* like the second, and the *seventh* like the first.

Played by a group of six children, a complete sequence might go like this:

Round 1

Player 1: I packed my grandmother's trunk with avocados.
Player 2: . . . avocados and bricks.
Player 3: . . . avocados, bricks, and cotton.
Player 4: . . . avocados, bricks, cotton, and devils.
Player 5: . . . avocados, bricks, cotton, devils, and earmuffs.
Player 6: . . . avocados, bricks, cotton, devils, earmuffs, and fans.

Round 2

Player 1: . . . avocados, . . ., earmuffs, fans, and *gorgeous gloves*.
Player 2: . . . avocados, . . ., fans, gorgeous gloves, and hot hens.
Player 3: . . . avocados, . . ., fans, gorgeous gloves, hot hens, and icy irons.
Player 4: . . . avocados, . . ., fans, gorgeous gloves, hot hens, icy irons, and jolly Junebugs.
Player 5: . . . avocados, . . ., fans, gorgeous gloves, hot hens, icy irons, jolly Junebugs, and keen kites.
Player 6: . . . avocados, . . ., fans, gorgeous gloves, hot hens, icy irons, jolly Junebugs, keen kites, and liquid lumps

Round 3

Player 1: . . avocados, . . ., fans, gorgeous gloves, . . . liquid lumps, and *Molly's mighty magnets*.
Player 2: . . . Neil's nice noodles.
Player 3: . . . Oliver's old ostrich.
Player 4: . . . Peter's playful penguin.
Player 5: . . . Quincy's quiet quoits.
Player 6: . . . Ruthie's rude rabbits.

Round 4

Player 1: . . . *Sweet Sam's silent swing*.
Player 2: . . . Tired Terry's ticklish trout.
Player 3: . . . Upset Ursula's ugly umbrella.
Player 4: . . . Vague Vinnie's violet valentine.
Player 5: . . . Whistling Willie's wild watermelon.
Player 6: . . . X-rayed Xavier's Xeroxed xylophone.

Round 5

Player 1: . . . *Yancy's young yams*.
Player 2: . . . Zachary's zig-zag zipper!

The dictionary and atlas may be consulted during this game if necessary, or the teacher may give hints for difficult letters like *X* and *Q*.

164. *Traveling.* This game is similar to "Grandmother's Trunk," but each child simply names a place and an object beginning with the same letter, not repeating those named before. For example: "I went to Allentown and took an adding machine." "I went to Boston and took a bicycle." "I went to Canada and took calendars."

165. *Categories.* A chart is placed on the blackboard listing several categories (such as animals, flowers, cars, girls' names, etc.) vertically, and the letters of any five-letter word (for example, SPARK) horizontally. The categories are read aloud to the children, one at a time. For each category, the children try to think of words beginning with each of the letters. (The sounds of the letters can be made by the teacher to remind the children of the sounds their words might begin with.) Do one category at a time, and use the letters from left to right.

	S	P	A	R	K
ANIMALS CARS NAMES FLOWERS	squirrel	puppy	alligator	rabbit	kangaroo

Later, vary this by doing all the categories for one letter, then going on to the next letter. The children take turns supplying a word in each category, beginning with each letter of the word at the top.

When the children understand the game, each one can make a chart on his own paper and play individually, with a time limit. Score can be kept by giving 1 point to a word that more than a third of the group has, 2 points to a word that one third or less of the group has, and 3 points for words no one else has. This game frequently leads to consultation of reference books to settle disputes.

166. *Similes.* Children try to think of the extreme cases of qualities described by familiar adjectives—for example, the *thinnest* thing they can think of, the *loudest* thing they can think of, the *hottest* thing they can think of. Then, using the simile form, they tell about something that is as *thin* as a_____, as *loud* as a_____, as *hot* as a_____. Some adjectives that lend themselves to this kind of activity are:

hot	warm	brave	high	lonely	cold	short
sad	tiny	tired	thin	helpful	hard	sticky
old	slow	mean	long	happy	loud	different
big	cool	angry	scary	rough	flat	surprising

(continued)

55

dry	ugly	pretty	quiet	funny	soft	slippery
wet	easy	bumpy	heavy	shiny	lazy	boring
new	deep	silly	sweet	proud	good	alike

167. *Yesterday, Today, Tomorrow.* The different forms of verbs are put onto cards and dealt to the children. A "book" is made with all the forms of one verb (e.g., *go, went, will go, going*). The game is played like "Go Fish," the children taking turns asking for forms of·verbs they need to complete their books, and taking from the center pile if the child they ask does not have the card they need. When a child has the cards for all four forms of a verb, he must give a sentence for each, and then put his book down. The winner is the player with the most books. The thirteen verbs suggested for this game are:

GO (go, went, will go, going)
TALK (talk, talked, will talk, talking)
SING (sing, sang, will sing, singing)
DRINK (drink, drank, will drink, drinking)
EAT (eat, ate, will eat, eating)
LAUGH (laugh, laughed, will laugh, laughing)
LEAD (lead, led, will lead, leading)
THINK (think, thought, will think, thinking)
ASK (ask, asked, will ask, asking)
BE (am, was, will be, being)
HAVE (have, had, will have, having)
GIVE (give, gave, will give, giving)
RUN (run, ran, will run, running)

When the children are thoroughly familiar with these, the past participle forms can be added (*have gone, have talked, have sung, have drunk, have eaten, have laughed, have led, have thought, have asked, have been, have had, have given, have run*), and five cards are needed to make a book.

168. *Hangman.* One child thinks of a word, or selects one from a reader. He writes the same number of dashes as there are letters in the word. The other players begin to guess the letters, one at a time. If the letter is in the word, the leader writes it above the appropriate dash, in as many places as it occurs in the word. Each letter that is guessed incorrectly is written to the side of the page (or chalkboard) so that incorrect guesses are not repeated. When an incorrect guess is made, the leader begins to draw a scaffold, and then a hanged man, one part at a time. If he completes the drawing before the others have guessed the word, he wins. If a player guesses the word before the man is hanged, that player becomes the hangman. (Details such as eyes, nose, mouth, hands, feet, and buttons can be added to the sequence shown in the illustration.)

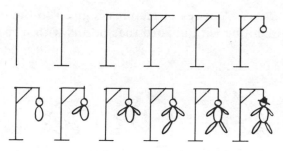

169. *"Light and Drum."* The leader selects a pair of homonyms—for example, *bear-bare*. He does *not* say them, but gives two or more exact definitions of the word—for example, "It is the name of an animal, and it means uncovered." The children guess the word. For those with a high degree of language ability, follow this with the more advanced and difficult game called "Light and Drum." A "light" is a light hint, and a "drum" is a strong hint. Children may ask for a light or a drum whenever they wish, while they are guessing. However, when a child knows or thinks he knows the answer, he does not give the answer; instead, he gives another hint. The game is played as follows: the leader defines the word in general terms, giving as many different meanings as possible. Using *bear-bare*, he might say, "It is an animal; it is uncovered; it is sometimes said of trees; it is a kind of hug; . . . ." Any other player who thinks he has guessed the word may raise his hand and continue the description of the word in either meaning, without naming it: "It is sometimes a rug; it is sometimes cinnamon or honey; . . . ." As each player thinks he knows the word, he adds different uses and descriptions of it. The leader indicates whether the descriptions fit or not. The game continues until everyone has guessed the word or has given up. A player who is having trouble can ask for a light or a drum from anyone who knows the word.

170. *Auditory Categories.* The teacher reads a list of unrelated words—for example, *car, chair, goldfish, sandwich, skirt, house*. Then the teacher calls on a child and says, "A pet." The child must reply with the name of a pet that the teacher had mentioned (in this case, *goldfish*). The teacher then says, "A place to live." Then, "Something to sit on." "Something to eat." "Something to ride in." "Something to wear." The number of items on the list and the breadth of the categories can be increased for more mature children.

171. *Greeting Card Dictionary.* Children are given word cards or strips to help them spell words they use in making greeting cards. They keep the cards or strips in a notebook or file box. New words are added as needed. Examples of words often used: *birthday, love, Christmas, happy, dear, Valentine's Day, Mother's Day, wish, congratulations, many happy returns, loving, son, daughter, friend.*

172. *Vocabulary Recall.* A series of pictures is given to the children, and they must name each one with a word that begins with a specified letter. (See Figure 1.)

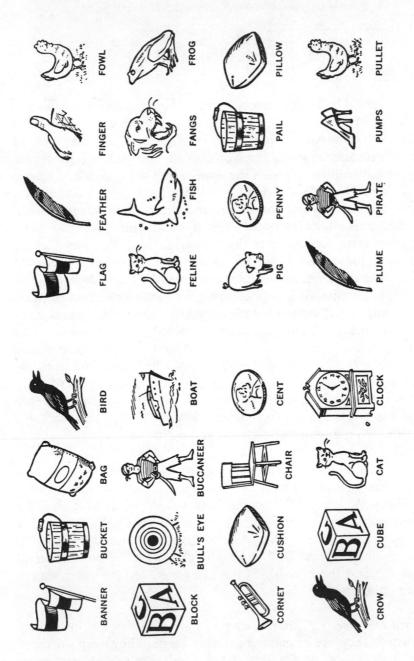

Figure 1. Reprinted by permission of S. G. Phillips, Inc., from *How to Raise Your Child's I.Q.*, by David Engler. Copyright © 1958 by S. G. Phillips, Inc.

173. *In the Manner of the Word.* One player chooses an adverb (like *softly, rapidly, sadly*) but doesn't tell what it is. The other players ask him to carry out various actions (e.g., *eat, dance, read, walk*) "in the manner of the word." Whoever guesses the adverb chooses the next one.

174. *Directions Test.* A very hard follow-the-directions sheet appears below. The teacher should try it himself before using it (with very advanced children), and be careful about arousing hostility on the part of the children. Some children enjoy this kind of activity, but others feel threatened by it.

Can You Follow These Directions?

1. Read everything before doing anything.
2. Write your name at the top of this paper
3. Make a circle around the title of this paper.
4. Draw three small squares at the upper right corner of this paper.
5. When you get to this point, stand up and say your name out loud.
6. Draw a triangle on the back of this page.
6. Put a circle in each corner of this paper.
8. If you have followed the directions so far, say "Yes!" out loud.
9. One direction is numbered wrong. Put a circle around the wrong number.
10. Now that you have read everything, follow only the first three directions.

175. *Rhyme Definitions.* This is a more advanced form of the Rhyme Game (§ 133). The leader begins by saying (for example) "I am thinking of a word that rhymes with *sky*." The guessers, in turn, try to guess the word by giving definitions of the word they think it is; for example, one player might say, "Is it the opposite of *low*?" The leader then says, "No, it is not *high*." The guessers must only define their words, not say them. If the leader cannot guess the word the guesser had in mind, he challenges him to tell it. If the guesser's word is not a real rhyme, the guesser is out. But if it really is a word that rhymes, then the leader must tell his word, and the guesser becomes the new leader. Or when someone guesses the correct word, that person becomes the new leader.

Children learning this game often have difficulty giving definitions without using the word, and try to pantomime. This should not be allowed (except as a variation of the game). The teacher can point out the *different ways of defining words*: (1) by synonyms, (2) by giving their opposites, (3) by using a formal dictionary definition, or (4) by describing the situation in which the word is used, as by saying "This is the word you use when you ask a question about a place" (*where*). The use of reference material like dictionaries and thesauruses should ordinarily be allowed in this game, except when it would slow it down too much. The reference books should be allowed only to find a good definition of a word the player has in mind, not to find a rhyming word.

176. *Dictionary Stories*. (For children who can read.) A dictionary is opened at random, and a child closes his eyes and points to a word. The word is written down, with its definition (by the teacher, usually). After five words have been selected in this manner, the child (or children, if several participate) must weave the words into a story. This can be conducted as an individual or group activity.

177. *True, False, Can't Tell*. The teacher makes a statement and calls on a child to tell whether it is true, or false, or if one can't tell. If the child responds correctly he gets a point. After some experience, or with older children, the child who responds correctly can give the next statement and call upon another child. If the answer is "Can't tell" (or " 'T'aint necessarily so!"), the child must say *why* one can't tell. Examples of statements in each category:

True	*False*	*Can't tell*
Christmas comes in December.	Christmas is in summer.	I got 20 Christmas cards.
Milk comes from cows.	Milk grows on trees.	Milk tastes good.
Bees can sting.	Bees ride bicycles.	This bee will sting you.
Fire is hot.	Ice is hot.	You need fire to cook.
Birds lay eggs.	Birds jump rope.	Birds are big.
Trees grow.	Trees walk.	Trees are green.
Babies cry.	Babies read books.	Babies are boys.
Cars can move.	Cars can talk.	Cars are small.
Men can laugh.	Men know everything.	Men are married.
Women can think.	Women can jump over a house.	Women are mothers.

6
Tactile Perception Skills

TACTUAL QUALITIES

178. Give the child something hard and something soft (e.g., a piece of wood and a piece of cotton). Teach the words "hard" and "soft" as he feels the objects while looking at them.

179. Have the child close his eyes. Put a soft material in his hand (cotton, sponge, clay, dough, plastic bag stuffed with old nylon stockings, etc.) or a hard material (wood, metal, rigid plastic, pottery, etc.). Have him tell by feel alone if the material is "hard or soft."

180. Repeat the procedures of §§178 and 179 with "rough or smooth," "warm or cool," "sharp or blunt," "sticky or slick."

181. The child closes his eyes, feels something, and classifies it according to as many of the above categories as are appropriate.

182. The child reaches into a paper bag which contains various objects, and guesses what material they are made of by touch.

183. The children make lists or scrapbooks of items in various categories of materials. For example, they might set up the category Hard Materials, with subsections such as wood and metal. Another category could be Rough Materials, subdivided into sandpaper, screening, and so on. The subsections could be illustrated with pictures cut from magazines.

184. Make a set of tactile cards, with the surfaces varying from rough sandpaper to soft, slick nylon. Some suggestions for materials: rough fabric, fur, satin, tweed, leather, suede, cotton, manila paper, glazed paper, and cellophane. The cards are then duplicated for texture, but not

for appearance (e.g., if one is red satin, make another of white satin, and make both small and large cards, square and round cards, etc.). The child matches the two sets by texture.

THREE-DIMENSIONAL FORMS

185. Show the child two blocks of different familiar shapes. Then he closes his eyes and receives one block, then the other. He must guess which is which. If he cannot distinguish between them, he looks. Later he identifies them inside a paper bag. With experienced players, more than two shapes can be used.

186. Common objects are concealed in a bag. One at a time, children put their hand in the bag and identify an object by touch. Good objects for this activity are pencils, blocks, paper clips, spoons, pebbles, pegs, and erasers.

187. The teacher pastes different shapes of thick felt on cardboard squares. The child feels them and names them with his eyes open; later, he names them by touch with his eyes closed.

SHAPES AND STENCILS

188. *Letters and Numbers.* The teacher writes letters and numbers on cardboard squares with glue and sprinkles it with sand (or cuts the letters or numbers out of sandpaper and pastes them on). Let the child look at the figure while he runs his fingers over it. Later he identifies the number or letter by touch alone. The teacher must be sure the figure is correctly oriented at first. Later on, the child can orient the figure himself, with his eyes closed.

189. Cut-out letters, numbers, and other shapes can be prepared by the teacher, first out of heavy cardboard, then oaktag. The child identifies them by touch alone, the teacher putting them into his hand behind his back. The oaktag needs to be handled very delicately, and children need lots of practice before they can be sensitive enough to identify oaktag figures.

190. *Stencil Shapes.* The teacher prepares stencil cut-outs of a circle, a square, a triangle, a diamond, and a rectangle. The children feel the shape and then draw what they have felt.

7
Olfactory Perception Skills

RECOGNITION

191. *Smell Box.* The teacher prepares a box containing various items with characteristic odors. The children close their eyes and try to identify various items by smell alone. Some items for this box might be coffee, chocolate, perfume, lemon, leather, newsprint (with fresh print on it), toothpaste, soap, a banana, paint, clay, olive oil, cheese, freshly cut wood, pine or balsam needles, cinnamon, nutmeg.

192. *What Do You Smell?* The teacher should call the attention of the children to different smells in the context of the day's activities, for example, the characteristic odor of bacon cooking, or of a car exhaust, or of freshly cut grass, or of honeysuckles or other fragrant flowers, or the odor of hot metal that rises when the heat first comes up into the radiators in the fall, or the odor in the air that precedes snow.

193. *What's Cooking?* The teacher prepares food that has a characteristic odor when being cooked. The children identify the single odors or combinations. If classroom cookery is not feasible, the school cafeteria might be used on occasion. Some good foods for this activity are bacon, coffee, lemonade, hamburger, popcorn, onions, garlic, cabbage, shrimp.

194. *Sniff Walk.* The teacher takes the children for a walk during the warm weather in such areas as woods, grassy areas, garages, restaurants, florist shops, bakeries, and other places with characteristic smells. The children comment on and try to identify smells.

195. *Herbs.* Children can rub herbs (dried or fresh) on their fingers and sniff them, selecting favorites. No more than two, one per hand, should be used on any occasion to avoid confusion. Some pleasant-smelling herbs

for this activity are spearmint, peppermint, chives, rosemary, basil, tarragon, thyme, dill, parsley, and marjoram. Spices can also be used for this activity.

196. *Perfume.* Different perfumes or toilet waters can be put on blotting paper strips and labeled. Children can learn to identify them by name or by characteristic odor. Perfumes and colognes are classified as floral, spicy, woody, and "modern" (blends); and commercial literature usually describes them in terms of these classifications. Their names sometimes reflect the type of scent. Lilac and rose are the most easily identified florals; spicy scents usually have names of spices.

RECALL

197. *How Did That Smell?* Classify smells as sweet, pungent, or putrid. The teacher should encourage the memory and description of smells of familiar objects such as one's puppy, the classroom, or a baby.

198. *Creative Writing.* The children could be assigned to write (or tell) about a time they have experienced and to describe it in terms of smell as well as sight and sound. In beginning this kind of activity, the teacher will find it helpful to narrow the children's choice of scenes to remember by offering suggestions such as "The First Thing in the Morning," "When I Sat Down to Dinner," or "On the School Bus."

8
Gustatory Perception Skills

RECOGNITION

199. *Let's Make a Treat.* Let children prepare (or help prepare) foods in the classroom: instant puddings, corn flakes or shredded wheat topped with applesauce and cream, popcorn, pancakes with syrup or honey, sandwiches (peanut butter and jelly, cheese, tuna, egg). Then let them eat and enjoy!

200. *Mystery Sandwich.* Make a sandwich and let the children identify it blindfolded, naming each ingredient. Use ingredients you know will be familiar and acceptable. (Combinations such as shredded carrot and raisin, or pineapple and mayonnaise, or mayonnaise with meat, would probably be strange to some children.)

201. *With and Without.* Tasting various foods with and without various condiments is another interesting idea for snack times. Some children don't know the taste of unsalted or un-ketchupped food!

202. *Taste Box.* (Cf. §191.) This should contain food items with characteristic tastes but less distinctive odors than the Smell Box items; this is partly compensated for by the fact that the texture of the food in the mouth is perceived as part of the taste. Use such varied items as hard candy, bread, cooked potato, mild cheese, salt, sugar, vinegar, and oil. Children must be reassured many times before they are willing to participate in this activity. Pleasant-tasting substances must be given, and the children must learn to trust that this will be the fact.

203. Have children identify common foods with their eyes closed. This encourages the use of combined taste and smell perception, since many foods cannot be identified by taste alone (a raw potato tastes like a raw apple, if the nose is held closed, for example).

204. *Menu Books*. Children can make these by cutting pictures of food out of magazines and putting them together to make good meals. The title page of the book should name the meal; other pages name its various dishes and illustrate them. Examples of interesting menus: My Birthday Dinner, Breakfast at Uncle Harry's House, Lunch at the Beach, Thanksgiving Dinner, My Favorite Snack, I Love Chicken, Supper for a Hot Day, Holiday Brunch.

205. *What Was It?* Children take turns describing the taste and texture of foods, letting other children guess what food is referred to.

206. *Restaurant Menus*. The teacher brings menus from local restaurants to school, and the children select meals from them. In some cases this activity might be followed up by a real visit to a restaurant if it can be arranged.

207. *Comparisons*. Encourage discussion of food likes and dislikes, descriptions of meals eaten, memories of tastes, and comparisons of tastes to deepen children's perception. Ask questions like "What exactly is the difference in taste between a hamburger and a hot dog? between a watermelon and a grape?"

208. *The Spice of Life*. Teach meal planning from the point of view of *variety of tastes* as well as nutritional balance. Have the children plan a breakfast, for example, that has "something sweet, something spicy, something salty, something sour." Plan a meal that includes something a little bitter. (Among foods having a somewhat bitter taste are endive, orange peel, and core of lettuce. Most people dislike a bitter taste, but sometimes it is pleasant in combination with a very sweet taste, as in candied orange peel or kumquats or bittersweet chocolate.)

9
Kinesthetic Perception and
Gross Motor Skills

The term "body image" describes a person's awareness of his own physical dimensions and position in space as compared to other phenomena he sees. For example, a child with a poor body image cannot judge how low to duck under a fence or whether he can fit into a designated area or container. He does not know "where he is" in space. Kinesthetic skills reinforce a child's body image—help him locate himself, judge his dimensions and position. It should be noted here, as was mentioned in Chapter 4, that kinesthetic skills strongly influence those visual skills that depend on all motor skills, both large and small.

This chapter includes a variety of *gross motor skill* activities. The reader will find many activities involving *small motor skills* elsewhere in this book— especially those in Chapter 4 on Form Perception, Visual Comparison, and Eye-Hand Coordination.

BASIC ACTIVITIES

Floor Exercises and Toe Touch[25]

209. *"Angels in the Snow."* The child lies on his back on the floor, his legs together, his arms at his sides. He moves both arms along the floor until they are above his head. At the count of "two" he returns them to his sides. The leg movement is done separately at first: At the count of "one," the child slides his legs apart, along the floor. At the count of "two," he brings them back together again. When the child can do arm and leg movements smoothly, he combines them: at the count of "one," his arms move out and up and his legs apart; at the count of "two," he

---

[25] Getman, *How to Develop Your Child's Intelligence.*

brings his arms and legs back to the starting position. Sometimes the words "open" and "close" make it easier for the child to follow the directions than "one" and "two."

210. *Trunk Lift.* The child lies face down with his stomach on a pillow, hands behind his head, clasped at his neck. He raises his trunk off the floor. If he cannot do this, the teacher can hold his feet down at first, until the back muscles are strengthened.

211. *Leg Lift.* The child lies face down, with his stomach on a pillow, his hands on the floor under his chin. He lifts one leg at a time as high as possible without rolling over onto his side. When he can lift each leg separately, he lifts both together. The teacher may help him at first by placing a sling under his ankles and pulling it to lift his legs for him; this will give him the feeling of the movement.

212. *Sit-ups.* The child lies on his back with hands clasped behind his neck. The teacher can hold his feet down if necessary. He sits up, then lies down again. A sling at the back of the child's neck may be necessary at first to help him feel the movement. This exercise is easier when it is done quickly. As the child gains skill in sitting up quickly, have him try to do it slowly and rhythmically, sitting up to a count of four and lying down to a count of four. Do not do too many of these at first—they lead to uncomfortable "Charley-horse" of the abdominal muscles if overdone.

213. *Bent-Knee Sit-ups.* The child lies on his back, with his knees bent and his feet almost touching his buttocks. The teacher holds his feet down as the child sits up. This exercise uses the abdominal muscles only, and is harder than regular sit-ups. The teacher may help the child with a sling at first. Go slowly with this exercise to prevent Charley-horse.

214. *Feet Lift.* The child lies on his back with a pillow under his hips. He lifts his feet with legs straight to a distance of ten inches above the floor, then holds them there as long as possible—aim for about ten seconds. He may have to begin this exercise by lifting one leg at a time, and he may need help from the teacher at first.

215. *Toe Touch.* The child stands, feet together, knees straight. He bends at the hips and touches his fingertips to his toes, holding the position for three seconds. If he cannot do this, have him touch his knees, and try to slide his fingers down his legs a little further each time he does the exercise.

Integration

Creeping and Crawling

Creeping and crawling activities are on a lower developmental level than walking, and they are helpful in establishing movement patterns that are bilateral. (Creeping and crawling are the same thing according to some dictionaries. But some authorities differentiate between them, using *creeping* to mean locomotion via hands and knees, and *crawling* to mean any other type of locomotion with the body face down on the floor. Still other authorities use the words in exactly the opposite way; so, to avoid confusion, we will use only the word *creep*, meaning to go along the floor on hands and knees.)

216. *Creeping Races.* The children imitate different animals that go on all fours—for example, turtles (creeping very slowly), dogs (creeping faster), and so on. They race to a goal.

217. *Creeping to Music.* The teacher plays the piano or a record, or beats out a rhythm on a drum, and the children creep to the beat. The right hand advances with the left knee, and the left hand with the right knee.

218. *Creeping Obstacle Course.* The room is set up so that the child must go *under* tables, *around* chairs, *over* boxes, *along* strings or narrow boards, *between* markers, *on* blocks, *up* and *down* steps, *forward, sideways,* and *backward.* This can be varied by having the child follow hand- and knee-shaped cut-outs along a course. Positional concepts and relationships are strengthened by the use of the positional word as the child performs the activity ("*Under* the table, then *around* the chair, then *over* the box," etc.).

Walking Obstacle Course

219. The activity described in §218 is done on the feet rather than on hands and knees. A ladder placed flat on the floor can also be used—the child walks, alternating feet, between the rungs, swinging the opposite arm forward with each step, turning his head to the side on which his leg is advancing.

Balance, Coordination, and Spatial Orientation

Balance Activities[26]

220. The child balances on his head first a ruler, then a yardstick, then a book.

---

[26] Suggested by Child Guidance Section, Optometric Extension Program Foundation, Inc., Duncan, OK 73533.

221. The children build structures with oversized blocks.

222. Have the children hop on one foot, then on the other.

223. *Balance Board.* A 12-inch-square board (¾-inch plywood) is mounted on a ½-inch piece of wood 2 inches by 2 inches, the ½ inch being the height the board is to be off the floor. The child stands on this and tries to balance. When he has learned to balance on this, the support can be raised from ½ to 1 inch, 1½ inches, and 2 inches. When the child is skillful in balancing, he can try to catch a ball, recite a poem, repeat number combinations, and so on, while in this position.

224. *Pogo Stick and Stilts.* Homemade stilts can be made by putting strong cord through holes in opposite sides of cans, and tying the cans onto the child's feet. Begin with soup cans, and later vary with large juice cans and narrow frozen-juice cans.

Activities with Equipment[27]

225. *Hoop Activities.* Rolling and hula-hooping (revolving the hoop on the hips by rhythmically moving the torso).

226. *Jump Board.* A board 8 feet long by 8 inches wide is placed on two low supports, one at either end. The child jumps up and down on the board. The wood has a natural springiness in it, which forces the child to adjust his balance.

227. *Jumping.* The child jumps over a rope, down from steps, from a box, or from the jump board.

---

[27] *Ibid.*

228. *Jungle Gym.* Climbing on a pipe jungle gym increases the child's perception of space and directionality, since he can climb in many different directions.

229. *Roller Skating and Ice Skating.*

230. *Self-propelled Swing.*

231. *Stunts:* somersaults, headstands (with legs held by the teacher), the wheelbarrow walk (walking on his hands, as his legs are held up by the teacher or another child), rolling across the room or down a hill. These help the child develop awareness of his body in relation to space.

232. *Stepping:* pacing so as to step on or to avoid the cracks in the sidewalk, stepping on one's own shadow, catching someone else's shadow with his feet. These activities help in control and direction.

233. *Seesaw.* This requires balance and leg activity to keep it going if the two weights are in good balance.

234. *Scooter, Tricycle, and Bicycle.* Riding any wheeled vehicle requires and develops gross motor skills in steering, keeping the wheels going, and balancing.

Games

235. Games to develop coordination and spatial orientation:
   A. *Coordination*
      Ball games: baseball, soccer, dodgeball, kickball,
         volleyball, newcomb, etc.
      Follow the Leader
      Bowling
      Bean Bag
      Shuffleboard
      Ring Toss (or Horseshoes)
   B. *Spatial orientation*
      Blindman's Buff
      Blindfold obstacle course
      Pin the Tail on the Donkey
      Walking a maze blindfolded
      Walking through a familiar room blindfolded

236. Exercises to develop strength, agility, flexibility:

> Push-ups
> Stationary running
> Scissors jump
> Astride jumps
> Deep knee bends
> Spread-eagle jumps (begin with deep
>   knee bend, jump in the air, feet wide
>   and legs straight, arms overhead,
>   then return to knee bend.)

MORE GAMES

237. *Handies* This game is played sitting around a table. The leader holds his fists on the table, thumbs up, and bounces them lightly three times, saying "One, two, three." He then makes various moves, using his fingers, palms, arms, and head and face to make patterns. The other children must copy each pattern when the leader says "Three." Children who make incorrect patterns are out, and the last one left becomes the next leader.

238. *Find the Treasure.* In this game children must follow verbal clues to find an object in the room. The walls of the room are labeled to indicate North, East, South, and West. The child begins by facing North. He is then given a series of instructions.

Example: *Turn East* (to his right); *walk three steps. Turn South* (right); *walk ten steps. Look high. Find a blue book. Open to page 46.* Etc.

239. *Body Imitation Games.* Games such as "Looby Loo," "Did You Ever See a Lassie?" and "Monkey See—Monkey Do" help young children become more aware of spatial relationships and develop body image and kinesthetic awareness.

240. *Funny Bones.* The phrases listed below are copied onto cards, and the cards are shuffled. The leader of the game calls out the phrases as the cards turn up. All the rest of the children work with partners, and carry out the directions in turn, one couple at a time. When the couples have completed one round of directions, another round starts. The object of the game, for each couple, is to maintain contact already made while waiting for their next direction and to keep their balance while making the new contact and maintaining the first. (Be warned: this can get very tricky and hilarious! You may or may not want to eliminate some of the more tortuous combinations: ear to ankle, nose to foot, shoulder to toe, . . . ?)

If six children are playing, the game might go like this:

First round

    "Finger to thumb"   *First couple*: One child puts finger to partner's thumb.

    "Knee to knee"   *Second couple*: One child puts knee against partner's knee.

    "Nose to knuckle"   *Third couple*: One child puts nose to partner's knuckle.

Second round

    "Shoulder to hip"   *First couple*: One child puts a shoulder to partner's hip, *maintaining* the finger-to-thumb contact already established.

    "Knuckle to ankle"   *Second couple*: One child puts a knuckle to partner's ankle, *maintaining* knee-to-knee contact.

(And so forth.)

Using 15 body parts (ear, nose, chin, shoulder, elbow, wrist, hand, finger, thumb, knuckle, hip, knee, ankle, foot, and toe) you can have a total of 120 combinations with no repeats (e.g., knuckle to hand and hand to knuckle):

ear to ear	nose to elbow	chin to knuckle	elbow to elbow
ear to nose	nose to wrist	chin to hip	elbow to wrist
ear to chin	nose to hand	chin to knee	elbow to hand
ear to shoulder	nose to finger	chin to ankle	elbow to finger
ear to elbow	nose to thumb	chin to foot	elbow to thumb
ear to wrist	nose to knuckle	chin to toe	elbow to knuckle
ear to hand	nose to hip	shoulder to shoulder	elbow to hip
ear to finger	nose to knee	shoulder to elbow	elbow to knee
ear to thumb	nose to ankle	shoulder to wrist	elbow to ankle
ear to knuckle	nose to foot	shoulder to hand	elbow to foot
ear to hip	nose to toe	shoulder to finger	elbow to toe
ear to knee	chin to chin	shoulder to thumb	wrist to wrist
ear to ankle	chin to shoulder	shoulder to knuckle	wrist to hand
ear to foot	chin to elbow	shoulder to hip	wrist to finger
ear to toe	chin to wrist	shoulder to knee	wrist to thumb
nose to nose	chin to hand	shoulder to ankle	wrist to knuckle
nose to chin	chin to finger	shoulder to foot	wrist to hip
nose to shoulder	chin to thumb	shoulder to toe	wrist to knee

(*continued*)

73

wrist to ankle	finger to finger	thumb to ankle	hip to foot
wrist to foot	finger to thumb	thumb to foot	hip to toe
wrist to toe	finger to knuckle	thumb to toe	knee to knee
hand to hand	finger to hip	knuckle to knuckle	knee to ankle
hand to finger	finger to knee	knuckle to hip	knee to foot
hand to thumb	finger to ankle	knuckle to knee	knee to toe
hand to knuckle	finger to foot	knuckle to ankle	ankle to ankle
hand to hip	finger to toe	knuckle to foot	ankle to foot
hand to knee	thumb to thumb	knuckle to toe	ankle to toe
hand to ankle	thumb to knuckle	hip to hip	foot to foot
hand to foot	thumb to hip	hip to knee	foot to toe
hand to toe	thumb to knee	hip to ankle	toe to toe

241. *Penny Ball.* Two students stand about six feet apart. A penny is placed on the floor between them. One child bounces the ball, trying to hit the penny. The ball is caught by the other child, who then bounces it back, again trying to hit the penny. They continue to take turns. One point is given for each time the ball hits the penny; and a score of 21 wins when the children have had the same number of chances. For younger students, a quarter, half-dollar, or silver dollar may be used. For very young children, a still larger target (a circle of aluminum foil or colored paper) can be used, and the teacher can reduce the size of the target gradually until a coin can be used.

242. *Human Tic-Tac-Toe.* A large tic-tac-toe grid is placed on the floor (each square about 12 inches by 12 inches) and children are used as the crosses and circles, so designated by wearing X or O taped to their shirt fronts. Two teams are selected, each with a captain. The captains take turns positioning their members on the grid. A more difficult version of this is to let the team members position themselves, since they must be able to imagine the grid because they cannot see all of it when they are in it (especially when other children are in it too).

243. *Slow Race.*[28] This race can be carried out by two children or by teams in relay. The object of the race is to be the last to reach the goal. The contestants must move toward the goal as slowly as they can, without deviating from the direction or stopping.

244. *Pass the Penny.* Children form a circle. The leader places a penny on his index finger. He carefully passes it to the next player's index finger, who passes it to the next, and so on. Anyone who drops the penny is out of the game, or loses a point. A variation of this is to alternate prone and supine positions of the hands in passing the penny.

---

[28] Suggested by activities in Bryant J. Cratty, *Active Learning: Games to Enhance Academic Abilities* (Englewood Cliffs, N.J.: Prentice-Hall, 1971).

245. *Walk-a-Maze.* A large maze is put on the floor (drawn on brown paper or marked off with tape), and children walk through to find the goal. For younger children, actual barriers (blocks or shoe boxes or the like) can mark the dead ends—or even all the lines—of the maze.

246. *Feel Where to Go.* Various shapes are drawn on the chalkboard. The teacher or leader draws one shape on a child's back with his finger, then says: "Hop!" The child must hop to the correct shape and point to it. The action directions can include jumping, skipping, walking, creeping, running, rolling, walking backward (looking over one's shoulder), skating, and swimming as well as hopping. A more advanced version of this game is to trace a letter, number, or word on the child's back, instead of a simple shape.

247. *Target Throw.* Various games can be played using a large feltboard target and a ping pong ball with Velcro glued to it. The Velcro will make the ball stick to the flannel when thrown with sufficient force. The target can have numbers on it, and children can be required to add or multiply the numbers hit in two successive throws. Or the target might have words on it, and the child may be required to use the word in a sentence. Or children might get different points for hitting different areas of the target, and keep score by adding or multiplying the point score by a particular number.

248. *Footprints/Handprints.* A series of right and left foot and hand shapes are cut out of cardboard and colored (right one color, left another color). The shapes are placed on the floor some distance apart. The children must go across the floor matching their hands and feet to the prints without losing their balance. Points can be awarded for the number of prints the child successfully negotiates.

249. *Kick It Out.* Two parallel lines are drawn on the floor. Empty half-pint milk cartons are placed about a foot apart on each line. The children are required to walk steadily between the lines kicking the cartons out of the path, those on the left side with the left foot and those on the right side with the right foot. After a warm-up session, the activity must follow a regular beat. This can be accomplished by music, or by a metronome, or by the teacher clapping hands.

An advanced variation of this activity is to vary the beat and have the child follow it.

250. *Match the Target.* Use quoits-like targets of different shapes and colors. (These can be made of wood or cardboard, with toilet paper tubes for pegs.) Children must toss an open shape to its matching target. The open shapes can be made of wire or pipecleaners.

A more advanced variation of this game is color coding and/or shape coding words (e.g., words beginning with certain consonant sounds, or certain parts of speech) and attaching them to the wire shapes, and attaching the corresponding symbol to the target.

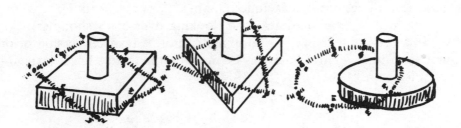

Bibliography

Barry, Hortense. *The Young Aphasic Child: Evaluation and Training.* Washington, D.C.: Alexander Graham Bell Association for the Deaf, 1961.

Bentzen, Frances, & Peterson, Wretha. "Educational Procedures with the Brain Damaged Child." In *Speech and Language Therapy with the Brain Damaged Child,* ed. by William T. Daley. Washington, D.C.: The Catholic University of America Press, 1962.

Bush, Wilma Jo, & Giles, Marian Taylor. *Aids to Psycholinguistic Teaching.* Columbus, Ohio: Charles E. Merrill Publishing Co., 1969

Carton, Aaron S. *Orientation to Reading.* Rowley, Mass.: Newbury House Publishers, Inc., 1976.

Child Guidance Section Publications. Optometric Expansion Program, Duncan, Oklahoma.

Connor, Frances P., & Talbot, Mabel E. *An Experimental Curriculum for Young Mentally Retarded Children.* New York: Teachers College Press, 1964.

Cratty, Bryant J. *Active Learning: Games to Enhance Academic Abilities.* Englewood Cliffs, N.J.: Prentice-Hall, 1971.

Cruickshank, William, *et al.,* eds. *A Teaching Method for Brain Injured and Hyperactive Children.* Syracuse, N.Y.: Syracuse University Press, 1975.

Cruickshank, William, & Hallahan, Daniel P., eds. *Perceptual and Learning Disabilities in Children, Vol. I (Psychoeducational Practices)* and *Vol. II (Research and Theory).* Syracuse, N.Y.: Syracuse University Press, 1975.

Duker, Sam. *Listening Bibliography.* 2nd ed. Metuchen, N.J.: The Scarecrow Press, 1968.

Engelmann, Siegfried. *Conceptual Learning.* Belmont, California: Dimension Publishing Co. in association with Fearon Publishers, 1969.

Engler, David. *How to Raise Your Child's I.Q.* New York: Ballantine Books, 1961.

Fernald, Grace. *Remedial Techniques in Basic School Subjects.* New York: McGraw-Hill, 1943.

Flavell, John H. *The Developmental Psychology of Jean Piaget.* New York: D. Van Nostrand Company, Inc., 1963.

Forrest, Elliott B. "Perspectives in Visual Function." In *Vision, Its Impact on Learning,* ed. by R. Wold. Seattle: Special Child Publications of the Seguin School, Inc., 1978.

Freidus, Elizabeth. "Methodology for the Classroom Teacher." In *The Special Child in Century 21,* ed. by Jerome Hellmuth. Seattle, Wash.: Special Child Publications of the Seguin School, Inc., 1964.

Frostig, Marianne. "Futures in Perceptual Training." In *Learning Disabilities: A Decade Ahead,* ed. by M. Krasnoff. Ann Arbor, Mich.: Institute for the Study of Mental Retardation and Related Disabilities, University of Michigan, Community Services Division, 1974.

_____ & Horne, David. *The Frostig Program for the Development of Visual Perception, Teacher's Guide.* Chicago: Follett, 1964.

Getman, Gerald N. "Concepts of Vision in Relation to Perception." In *Learning Disabilities: A Decade Ahead,* ed. by M. Krasnoff. Ann Arbor, Mich.: Institute for the Study of Mental Retardation and Related Disabilities, University of Michigan, Community Services Division, 1974.

_____; *How to Develop Your Child's Intelligence.* Luverne, Minn: Author, 1958.

_____; Kane, E.; Halgren, M.; & McKee, G. *Developing Learning Readiness.* Manchester, Mo.: Webster Division, McGraw-Hill, 1968.

Gibson, Eleanor J. *Principles of Perceptual Learning and Development.* Englewood Cliffs, N.J.: Prentice-Hall, 1969.

Goodfriend, Ronnie S. *Power in Perception for the Young Child: A Comprehensive Program for the Development of Pre-Reading Visual Perceptual Skills.* New York: Teachers College Press, 1972.

Goodman, Kenneth S., & Niles, Olive S. *Reading: Process and Program.* Urbana, Ill.: National Council of Teachers of English, 1970.

Hagin, Rose A.; Silver, Archie A.; & Kreeger, Henrietta. *Search and Teach.* New York: Walker Publishing Co., Inc., 1976.

Hammill, Donald P., & Bartel, Nettie R., *Teaching Children with Learning and Behavior Problems.* 2nd ed. Boston: Allyn and Bacon, Inc., 1978.

Haring, Norris G., & Miller, D. "Precision Teaching in Regular Junior High School Classrooms." In *Instructional Alternatives for Exceptional Children,* ed. by E. Deno. Reston, Va.: Council for Exceptional Children, 1973.

Hays, B. M., & Pereira, E. R. *The Fourth "R": Remembering.* Los Angeles: Instructional Equipment and Materials Distributors, 1977.

Hewett, Frank M., & Forness, Steven. *Education and the Exceptional Learner.* Boston: Allyn and Bacon, 1974.

Hunt, J. McVickers. *Intelligence and Experience.* New York: Ronald Press, 1961.

Jolles, Isaac. "A Teaching Sequence for Training of Visual and Motor Perception," *American Journal of Mental Deficiency,* 1958, 63: 252-255.

Karnes, Merle B. *Helping Young Children Develop Language Skills: A Book of Activities.* Rev. ed. Arlington, Va.: The Council for Exceptional Children 1973.

Kephart, Newell C. *The Slow Learner in the Classroom.* 2nd ed. Columbus, Ohio: Charles E. Merrill, 1971.

Kirk, Samuel A.; McCarthy, J. J.; & Kirk, W. *The Illinois Test of Psycholinguistic Abilities.* Rev. ed. Urbana, Ill.: University of Illinois Press, 1968.

_____ & McCarthy, Jeanne McRae, eds. *Learning Disabilities: Selected ACLD Papers.* Boston: Houghton-Mifflin Co., 1975.

Knoblock, Hilda, & Pasamanick, Benjamin, eds. *Gesell and Amatruda's Developmental Diagnosis: The Evaluation and Management of Normal and Abnormal Neuropsychologic Development in Infancy and Early Childhood.* 3rd ed., rev. and enl. New York: Harper and Row, 1975.

Listening and Speaking—K-3—A Packet for Teachers. New York: The University of the State of New York, State Education Department, Bureau of English Education/Bureau of Elementary Curriculum Development. Undated.

Lyon, Reid. "Auditory-Perceptual Training: The State of the Art," *Journal of Learning Disabilities,* 1977, 10:564-572.

Magdol, Miriam Sper. *Perceptual Training in the Kindergarten.* San Rafael, Calif.: Academic Therapy Publications, 1971.

Mallett, Jerry J. *Classroom Reading Games Activities Kit.* New York: The Center for Applied Research in Education, Inc., 1975.

Mauser, August J. *Assessing the Learning Disabled: Selected Instruments.* 2nd ed. San Rafael, Calif.: Academic Therapy Publications, 1977.

Monroe, Marion. *Growing into Reading.* Chicago: Scott, Foresman, 1951.

Montessori, Maria. *The Montessori Method.* New York: Frederick Stokes Co., 1912.

Myklebust, Helmer R., ed. *Progress in Learning Disabilities, Vols. I, II,* and *III.* New York: Grune and Stratton, 1968, 1970, 1975.

Oakland, T., & Williams, F. *Auditory Perception.* Seattle: Special Child Publications of the Seguin School, Inc., 1971.

Piaget, Jean. *The Language and Thought of the Child.* 2nd ed. Cleveland: World Publishing Co. (Meridian Books), 1955.

Platts, Mary E. *Spice: Suggested Activities to Motivate the Teaching of the Primary Language Arts.* Rev. ed. Stevensville, Mich.: Educational Service, Inc., 1973.

Redl, Fritz. *When We Deal With Children.* New York: The Free Press (a Division of the Macmillan Co.), 1966.

Romberg, Jenean, & Rutz, Miriam. *Art Today and Every Day: Classroom Activities for the Elementary School Year.* West Nyack, N.Y.: Parker Publishing Co., 1972.

Rosenfeld, Sam. *Thirty Days to a Higher I.Q. for Your Child.* New York: Crown, 1961.

Russell, David; Karp, Etta; & Mueser, Anne Marie. *Reading Aids Through the Grades.* 2nd rev. ed. New York: Teachers College Press, 1975.

Russell, David, & Russell, Elizabeth. *Listening Aids Through the Grades.* New York: Teachers College Press, 1960.

Slingerland, Beth H. *Slingerland Screening Tests for Identifying Children with Specific Language Disability. Form D.* Cambridge, Mass.: Educators Publishing Service, 1974.

Smith, Frank. *Comprehension and Learning: A Conceptual Framework for Teachers.* New York: Holt, Rinehart and Winston, 1975.

Staats, A. W. *Learning, Language and Cognition.* New York: Holt, Rinehart and Winston, 1968.

Strauss, Alfred, & Lehtinen, Laura. *Psychopathology and Education of the Brain Injured Child, Vol. I.* New York: Grune and Stratton, 1947.

Strauss, Alfred, & Kephart, Newell C. *Psychopathology and Education of the Brain Injured Child, Vol. II.* New York: Grune and Stratton, 1955.

Valett, Robert E. *The Remediation of Learning Disabilities.* Belmont, California: Fearon Press, 1967.

Van Witsen, Betty. *Teaching Children with Severe Behavior/Communication Disorders.* New York: Teachers College Press, 1977.

Wagner, Guy; Hosier, Max; & Blackman, Mildred. *Listening Games: Building Listening Skills with Instructional Games.* Rev. ed. New York: Teachers Publishing Division, Macmillan Publishing Co., Inc., 1970.

Appendix
PAPER FOLDING

The figures described on the following pages are all constructed from square paper unless otherwise noted. To square ordinary typing paper, or other rectangular paper, bring one short edge of the paper over to a long edge, by a diagonal fold from the corner, and crease. Cut off the paper lying outside the triangle thus formed.

The best paper for these figures is Japanese origami paper, which is obtainable in many local shops. Typing paper and construction paper can be used, but they are stiffer and more difficult to handle.

Another advantage of origami paper is that, being coated on one side only, it has two clearly different sides. Unless otherwise instructed, begin each figure with the coated side down.

You will get the best results if you fold very carefully and exactly and make all creases very sharp.

BASIC FOLDS

1. Book Fold

The left edge of the paper is brought to the right edge, and a crease is made in the center of the paper, so that it opens like a book. Some people find it easier to bring the bottom edge to the top edge, make the crease horizontally, then turn the paper so that it opens like a book.

2. Window Fold

Make the book fold; open the paper and make another fold perpendicular to the one just made, so that the opened paper has a cross in the center, all folds facing in.

3. Diagonal Fold

The lower left corner is brought to the upper right corner, and the paper creased diagonally.

4. Double Diagonal Fold

Make the diagonal fold; open the paper and make a second one using the other two corners.

5. Kite Fold

Make one diagonal fold. Open the paper, and bring up the lower edge of the paper so that it lies along the diagonal fold. Crease. Bring the left edge of the paper to the diagonal fold. Crease.

6. Checkerboard Fold

Begin with the window fold. Open the paper. Bring the top edge to the center crease, and the bottom edge to the center crease. Crease. Open up the paper. Make a one-quarter rotation of the paper and repeat.

7. Tent Fold

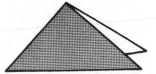

Make the double diagonal fold. Open the paper and turn it over. Make a book fold. Open and turn over the paper. Pinch up on the diagonals, letting the book fold fall to the inside.

8. Handkerchief Fold

Make the window fold. Open and turn over the paper. Make the diagonal fold. Open and turn over the paper. Pinch up on the window folds, letting the diagonal fold fall to the inside.

FIGURES

House

Make the window fold (Basic Fold No. 2). Open the paper. Bring top right and left corners to the center of the cross. Turn the paper over. It is now shaped like a house. Doors, windows, and chimney can be pasted on.

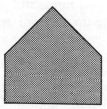

Envelope

Make the window fold (Basic Fold No. 2), and open the paper. Bring all four corners to the center and crease. Open up one corner. Put cellophane tape on the inside at the point where the three remaining corners meet.

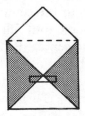

Standing Picture Frame

Begin with the coated side up. Make the window fold (Basic Fold No. 2). Open the paper. Bring all four corners to the center and crease. Turn the paper over and bring the four new corners to the center and crease. Turn over again. Lift each corner from the center and fold back to meet the outer corners. Draw or paste a picture in the center. This figure will stand if two adjacent large triangles at the back are suitably angled out.

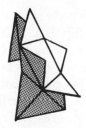

Basket

Make the window fold (Basic Fold No. 2), and open the paper. Bring all four corners to the center. Turn the paper over and bring the new corners to the center. Turn the paper over again and fold the top right corner to the bottom left corner. Open this fold and crease on the same line backward. Open again, and rotate the figure so that an uncreased corner is pointing downward. Lift the two side squares, with the fold lines, and pinch together along the crease, letting the bottom square come up and fall against the top square. Fasten a strip of paper for a handle between the front and back points at the top.

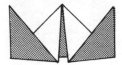

Tent

Make a double diagonal fold (Basic Fold No. 4). Open paper. Turn paper over and make a book fold (Basic Fold No. 1). Open up. Turn paper over again and bring the four corners to the center. Crease. Open up. Pinch up on the diagonal folds, letting the book fold fall to the inside. Bring the apex of the triangle to the base line at the center. Bring in the top flaps of the two side points to meet it (a). Open up these three folds. Bring the center point of the top flap of the base line to the apex, pushing down on the creases you have just made, to get a house shape (b). Turn over and repeat on the other side. Fold up the tent flaps at the center so that there is an entrance to the tent (c). This figure will stand.

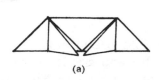

(a)

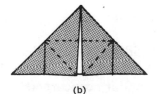

(b)

(c)

Bookmark or Mounting Corner

Make the tent fold (Basic Fold No. 7). Lay the figure down with the apex of the triangle at the top. Bring the top flap of the lower right hand corner to the apex. Crease. Turn the figure over. Bring the lower left corner to the apex and crease. Slip your fingers between the front and back sections. Bring the two front sections together and the two back sections together. Lay the resulting figure down flat and sharpen the creases. The little pocket formed will fit nicely on the corner of a page as a bookmark.

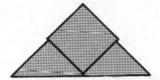

Balloon

Make the tent fold (Basic Fold No. 7). Lay the figure down with the apex of the triangle at the top. Bring the top flap of the lower right-hand corner to the apex. Crease. Bring the top flap of the lower left-hand corner to the apex. Crease. Turn the figure over and repeat. Bring the top flap of the new right corner to the midline. Crease. Repeat with the new left corner. Turn the figure over and repeat. Tuck the little points at the top into the little pockets of the triangles on the right and left sides (a). Turn over and repeat. Hold the figure gently and blow into the hole at the bottom. It will expand into a cube-shaped balloon (b). This figure makes a nice Christmas tree ornament.

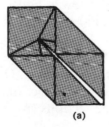
(a)

(b)

Butterfly

Make the tent fold (Basic Fold No. 7). Lay the figure down with the apex of the triangle to the top. Bring the upper flap of the lower right-hand corner to the apex. Crease. Bring the upper flap of the lower left-hand corner to the apex. Crease. Bring the right-hand point of the triangle that you have just made to the midline. Crease. Bring the left point to the midline. Crease. Bring the two front sections together and the two back sections together. Hold the front sections together, and let the back sections fall apart slightly. Pipe cleaner or wire antennae can be fastened to the butterfly's head.

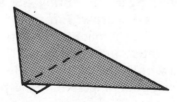

Drinking Cup

Make the diagonal fold (Basic Fold No. 3). Lay the paper down with the apex of the triangle to the top. Bring the lower right-hand corner about two thirds of the distance up along the left edge (a). Crease. Turn the figure over. Bring the new lower right-hand corner to the point where the other corner was folded in. Crease. Tuck the top flap into the little pocket. Turn over and repeat (b). This cup will hold water, if made of waxed paper or typing paper.

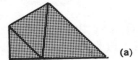 (a)   (b)

Bench

Make the checkerboard fold and open up (Basic Fold No. 6). Fold the top edge to the bottom edge. Fold the upper right square in half diagonally toward the center. Open up that fold. Repeat on the left. Lift the upper flap of the lower right-hand square and lay it flat on the square to its left. The square above this can then be pushed so that the lower half of it lies flat, and the upper half is folded back along the diagonal crease in this square and in the upper right-hand square. Repeat on the left side (a). Fold the two center squares of the lower section up so that the bottom edge meets the top edge. Fold the side sections to meet at the vertical midline. Open the side sections so that they stand at right angles to the center section. Lower the top flap gently so that it rests between the two side sections (b). This figure will stand.

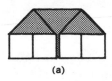
(a)

(b)

Fish

Make the checkerboard fold (Basic Fold No. 6). Open. Make the double diagonal fold. Open. Fold in the first row on the right-hand side and the top row, holding on to the upper right corner and pulling it out to the right (a). Repeat on the bottom, and on the top and bottom of the left side, until you have an elongated six-sided figure (b). Bring the upper right corner of the square to the center and crease sharply. Lift the triangle that is now lying on the lower right square and fold it back against the upper square. Fold the lower right corner to the center, and bring down the triangle to lie against it. Turn the figure over. Draw on eye (c). You can give your fish a funny face by opening its mouth, slipping your fingers into the pockets and bending them slightly apart.

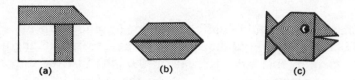

(a)   (b)   (c)

Boat

Fold down about a quarter of an inch at the top and at the bottom of the paper. Bring the new top edge to the new bottom edge, crease, and open up the paper. Bring the new top and bottom edges to the center fold. Bring down the top right hand corner so that the top right hand edge lies along the horizontal center line. Crease sharply. Do the same with the other three corners. Bring the upper left edge to the center horizontal line. Repeat with the lower left edge (a). Bring the top edge that lies parallel to the center fold down to meet the center. Crease very sharply. Repeat with the bottom edge. Fold the whole figure in half backward along the center fold. Slip your thumbs into the two channels, and, holding the folds closed with your forefingers against your thumbs, beginning at one end, carefully turn the figure inside out. Sharpen the creases that give the bottom of the boat its shape (b).

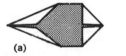   

(a)   (b)

Finger Puppet

Use a rectagular sheet of paper about the size of typing paper. Fold in half the long way. Open up. Bring both long sides to the center fold. Fold the whole figure in half along the center fold. Fold in half the short way. Open this fold and bring the two ends to this fold. Fold in half backward. Lay down so that the open ends are at the tip. Draw eyes and a nose on the top layer. Open up and draw teeth and tongue in the center two sections. Fold together again and slip your forefinger and middle finger into the inner pocket under the eyepiece and your thumb into the inner pocket below the lower mouth piece. The mouth opens and closes when you open and close your fingers. This basic figure can become a horse, a dragon, a person, a rabbit—by varying the features—and by adding ear pieces, yarn hair, or other individual variations.

87

Fox Finger Puppet

Make the checkerboard fold (Basic Fold No. 6), and open up. Fold the top edge to the bottom edge. Fold the upper right square in half diagonally toward the center. Open up that fold. Repeat on the left. Lift the upper flap of the lower right hand square and lay it flat on the square to its left. The square above this can then be pushed so that the lower half of it lies flat and the upper half is folded along the diagonal crease in this square and in the upper right hand square. Repeat on the left side (a). Fold the first line of squares on the right underneath, and the first line of squares on the left underneath, leaving the two center sections. The figure now has two squares at the bottom and three triangles at the top. Bring the right hand edge of the lower right hand square up to the horizontal center line. Turn over and do the same to the lower left hand square. Turn over again. Fold the lower left edge up on a diagonal line extending from the middle of the left side to the lower right corner (b). Turn figure over and repeat on the left side. Now fold the lower section up against the upper section folding along the horizontal midline. Turn figure over and repeat (c). Put your forefingers into the pocket, and your thumbs on the outside against the crease. Push in with your thumbs until the figure collapses into two smaller pockets. Slip your thumb into one pocket and your forefinger into the other pocket, and wiggle to make the mouth open and close (d). Draw eyes.

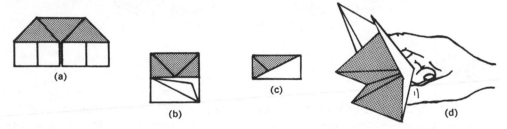

(a) (b) (c) (d)

Box

Use rectangular paper rather than square paper for this figure, or simply cut a strip off one side of an origami sheet. Fold in half along the long dimension. Open up and fold both long sides to the middle crease. Then fold in half backward along the short dimension. Holding the paper so that the folded edge is at the top, bring the top right hand corner to the center crease. Repeat on the left, then fold down along the bottom of the triangle you have just made. Open up these three folds. Lift the top layer at the lower center points and fold back at the same time along the little diagonal creases you have just made at the top. Bring up to lie flat against the top section and flatten out (a). Do the same on the reverse side. Fold the top right and left flaps to the center (b). Turn the figure over and repeat. Fold the top edge to the top of the little

88

triangles in the lower section then fold over again. Repeat on the reverse side. Slip your thumbs into the pockets and gently open out the box (c).

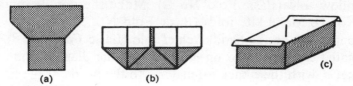

(a)   (b)   (c)

Pinwheel

Make double diagonal folds (Basic Fold No. 4). Open out. Bring two opposite corners to the center. Turn the paper over and bring the other two corners to the center. Repeat these two steps on the new, smaller square. You now have a figure with two triangular flaps facing you. Underneath the upper left of the top triangle is a little square. Pull the lower left corner of this square out to the right (a). Pull the lower corner out to the left (b). Turn the figure over and rotate ¼ turn. Repeat, as above, except that the top one goes to the left, and the lower one to the right (c). Flatten the figure. Tape the center on both sides, put a pin through the center and mount on the end of a pencil, through the eraser, or on a stick. It will spin when you blow into the sails.

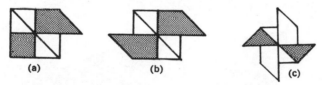

(a)   (b)   (c)

Paper Napkin Water Lily

This figure can also be made of tissue paper or other soft, thin paper. Open the napkin. If not already folded, make the window fold (Basic Fold No. 2). Bring the four corners to the center and crease. Bring the four corners of the new square to the center and crease. Repeat this step once more. Turn the figure over and repeat once on the reverse side. Tape down these four points. Place a glass or sturdy paper cup in the center of the figure. Reach underneath and bring up one of the folded corners, turning it inside out as you bring it up to the glass. Bring up the other three corners in the same way (a). Now bring up the next four corners in the same way. Bring up the four single triangles in the same way (b). (Note: if you use tissue paper, work with a square of about 18-20 inches, and fold four times on the first side instead of three. This will result in a fuller water lily.)

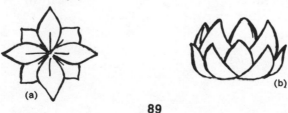

(a)   (b)

Wing-Flapping Bird

Make the window fold (Basic Fold No. 2). Make the double diagonal fold (Basic Fold No. 4). Make kite folds (Basic Fold No. 5) on all four corners. Open up the paper. Make the handkerchief fold (Basic Fold No. 8). You will see four elongated triangles, two on each side of the diagonal line (a). Push the outer triangles, with their back extensions, to the inside of the figure. Turn over and repeat. You now have a kite-shaped "handkerchief" (b). Lift the top flap of the bottom section of the kite and fold it up flat against the upper section of the kite, producing a tall diamond-shaped figure. Turn over and repeat (c). Bring lower right edge to the center and corner crease. Repeat on the left side. Turn over and repeat (d). Bring the lower right leg of the diamond up between the front and back sections, reversing the crease (e). Repeat with the lower left leg. Pull the large triangles out and down on both sides, expanding the body of the bird. Slip your thumb into the channel of the left long narrow triangle near the apex, and press down with your forefinger at the apex, turning it inside out, reversing the crease. This makes the head of the bird (f). Holding the bird just below the neck, at the breast with your left hand, pull the tail gently in and out, with your right hand. The wings will flap.

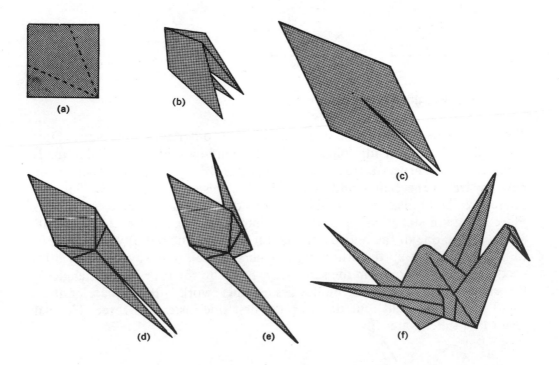

Newspaper Cap

Begin with tabloid newspaper, or easel paper. Make a square about 15 to 18 inches on a side. Make the double diagonal fold. Bring the four corners to the center. Turn over and repeat. Turn over and repeat again. Open up so that any two opposite corners are folded into the center (a). Place the figure so that the points are at the top and bottom. You will see, on the sides, two little triangles outlined by the folds (A and B) and, in the center, two more triangles at the tips of the corners (A' and B'). Pick up the two sides and proceed as though you were going to lay triangle A on A' and B on B'. While doing this, pick up the top point of the figure and bring it forward (b). Bring point C down to point D and crease along the fold already there (c). When this portion is folded down, you will see a square outlined by folds. Fold in the two sides and the bottom of the square, so the points meet in the center (d). Then fold the bottom edge of the square up to the top edge (e). Holding this folded portion down with one finger, turn the whole figure around, so that the point is now at the top. Repeat all the operations shown in illustrations "b" through "e." Then take hold of the two little tabs on top and open up the figure gently (f). Tuck one tab inside the cap and leave the other out, as a visor (g). Tape down the edges, if necessary. If this figure is made of stiff paper, the edges will stay flat, especially if you make the creases *very* sharp.

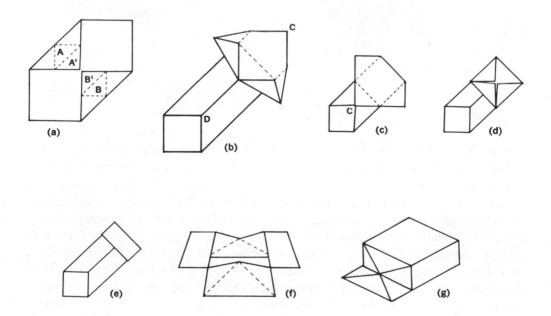

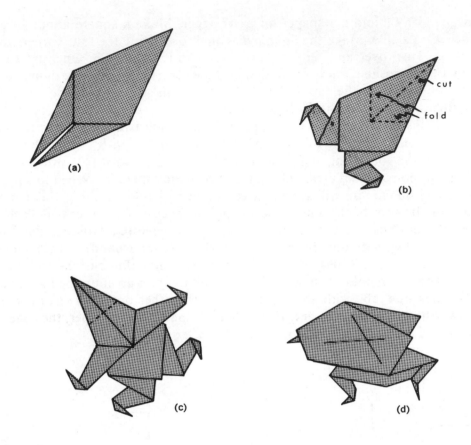

(a)

cut

fold

(b)

(c)

(d)

Frog

Make the window fold (Basic Fold No. 2), then the double diagonal fold
(Basic Fold No. 4). Make the kite fold (No. 5) on all four corners. Open up.
Make the handkerchief fold (Basic Fold No. 8). You will see four elongated
triangles, two on each side of the diagonal line. Push the outer triangles with
their back extensions to the inside of the figure. Turn over and repeat. Lift the
top flap of the bottom section of the kite and fold it up so that it lies flat
against the top section. Turn over and repeat. Lift the upper flap of the left
section and place it on the right section. Turn over and repeat. Lay the figure
down so that the two long triangles point down and the tail of the kite-shaped
section points up (a). Fold up the lower left and right triangles. Fold the
points down (b). Cut down and fold the "arms" out. Fold the arms a second
time, turning them up, and fold down the tip of the top triangle (c) so that the
point tucks under the front leg piece. Turn the figure over (d). If you tap his
tail, he will jump.

Shrimp

Make the kite fold (Basic Fold No. 5). Bring the long folded edges into the center and fold down (a), making a narrower "kite" shape. Then bring the two top edges into the center and fold down (b). Next, fold the top point down and up again, and cut a small triangle out of the second fold (c). Flatten the shape out to the original kite shape and cut up along each long side almost to the folded-in edges that run across the figure (d). These narrow strips are the shrimp's feelers. Put the figure back together along the same folds to match (c) again, and fold the feelers back up through the little hole (e). Next, turn the figure over and make four or five "step" folds down the back (f). Fold the entire figure exactly in half (g), and then gently pull at each fold (h) to create the curve in the shrimp's tail section. Fold the two feelers back, and the shrimp is completed (i).

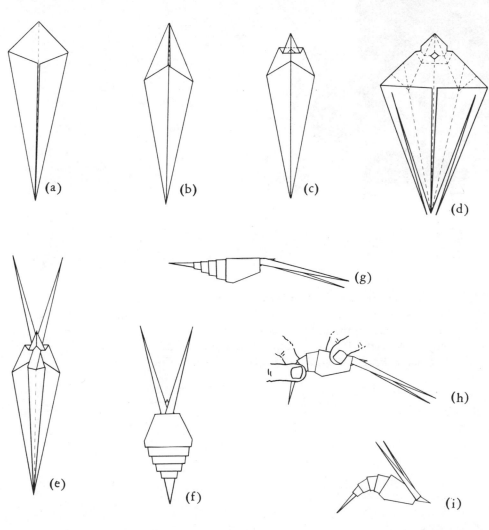

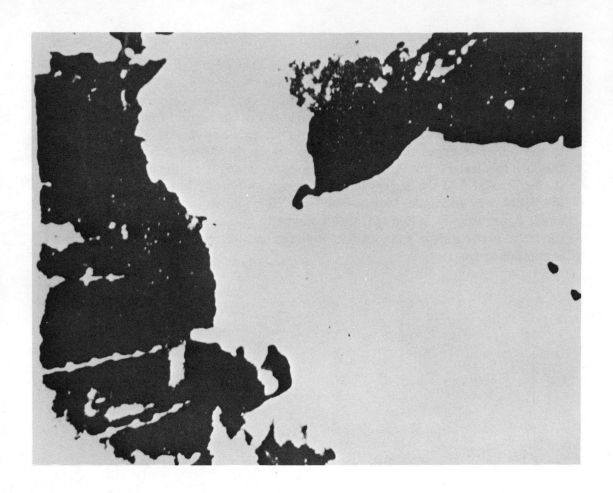

This is the picture that appeared at the beginning of the book. When you first look at it, you will not be able to distinguish much. This is, in fact, a picture of a cow, as becomes clear on the opposite page. "Mystery Picture.": reprinted, courtesy of the Optometric Extension Program Foundation, Inc., Duncan, OK 73533.

Now the cow can be clearly seen. Look at it carefully. Then look back to the picture at the left. When you reach the point where you can see the cow in *that* version of the picture, you have completed this exercise in perception. "Solution" to "Mystery Picture": adapted from original, courtesy of the Optometric Extension Program Foundation, Inc., Duncan, OK 73533

Index to Activity Topics and Titles

NOTE: References are to activity numbers, not page numbers. Activity titles are in *italics*.